CAREER SKILLS LIBRARY

Finding
A Job

CAREER SKILLS LIBRARY

Communication Skills

Finding A Job

Leadership Skills

Learning the Ropes

Organization Skills

Problem Solving

Professional Ethics and Etiquette

Research and Information Management

Teamwork Skills

FERGUSON
CAREER SKILLS LIBRARY

Finding
A Job

Ferguson Publishing
An imprint of Infobase Publishing

Finding A Job

Ferguson
An imprint of Infobase Publishing
132 West 31st Street
New York NY 10001

Library of Congress Cataloging-in-Publication Data

Finding a job.
    p. cm.
    Includes bibliographical references and index.
    ISBN-13: 978-0-8160-8104-2 (hardcover : alk. paper)
    ISBN-10: 0-8160-8104-2 (hardcover : alk. paper) 1. Job hunting. 2. Occupations. 3. Vocational guidance. I. Ferguson Publishing.
    HF5382.7.F55 2009
    650.14—dc22
                                        2009010179

Ferguson books are available at special discounts when purchased in bulk quantities for businesses, associations, institutions, or sales promotions. Please call our Special Sales Department in New York at (212) 967-8800 or (800) 322-8755.

You can find Ferguson on the World Wide Web at http://www.fergpubco.com

Text design by David Strelecky, adapted by Erik Lindstrom
Cover design by Takeshi Takahashi
First edition by Joe Mackall
Composition by Mark Lerner
Cover printed by Yurchak Printing, Landisville, Pa.
Book printed and bound by Yurchak Printing, Landisville, Pa.

Printed in the United States of America

This book is printed on acid-free paper.

CONTENTS

INTRODUCTION

After years of hard work in school, you're nearly done. You're about to graduate from high school or college and enter the workforce. Your life is changing, and it is exciting! You'll control your own destiny by choosing a career path, making new friends, learning new skills, and becoming a productive member of society. You're free. Well, at least sort of. Although you are shedding many of the old things in your life, you'll quickly learn that you will face new responsibilities and challenges.

It's time to take all of that education you received and find a career. Note that we said "career," not "job." A *job* is simply something you go to every day so you can pay your rent and cable television bill. It offers few advancement opportunities and little excitement. A *career,* on the other hand, is a rewarding occupation that offers the potential for advancement and higher earnings if you do a good job. It provides you with the chance to grow and develop your skills and gain confidence in yourself and your abilities. In short, a career makes you want to jump

HOT MAJORS

According to the Collegiate Employment Research Institute's *Recruiting Trends 2008–09* survey, demand is strongest for graduates with the following majors:

- Accounting
- Agribusiness
- Agricultural sciences
- Business administration
- Civil engineering
- Computer science
- Electrical engineering
- Environmental sciences
- Health technicians (all)
- Logistics/supply chain
- Marketing
- Mathematics
- Mechanical engineering
- Nursing

out of bed each morning before the alarm clock goes off so you can get to work early. (You know you have a job if you keep hitting the snooze button on the alarm clock and dread your every working minute.)

Now for the hard part: finding a career. The economic recession has hit American workers hard. Top companies have laid off hundreds of thousands of employees, and even companies that have avoided layoffs are refraining from adding too many new workers. This may seem daunting, but it's important to know that if you have good skills and a positive attitude, and know how to conduct a job search, you will eventually find a rewarding career.

People who work sitting down get paid more than people who work standing up.

—Ogden Nash, American humorist and poet

Have you ever heard people say, "Looking for a job is a job in itself"? This is often true. It takes time, planning, careful research, and dedication to find a good career. This book aims to provide you with the tools, the resources, and the information you need to land your dream job. It will provide the tools to help you stand out from the millions of other new graduates pounding the pavement looking for work. In this book, we'll look at some of the key job-search and career exploration tools, including how to:

- Match your personality, interests, and skills with a career

- Gain experience through internships, externships, and other experiential opportunities

- Research career options

- Network and tap into the hidden job market

- Write effective cover letters, resumes, and other job-search materials
- Apply for a job

Once you are asked to interview for a job, there are many things to remember and do to prepare. To ensure that you're successful once the interview process begins, this book also will provide you with detailed information about what to do before, during, and after the job interview; how to assess a job offer; and, if hired, what to do on your first day on the job and beyond. So what are you waiting for? Turn the page to start the next chapter of your life: finding a job!

1

WHO AM I? MATCHING YOUR PERSONALITY, INTERESTS, AND SKILLS WITH A CAREER

Casey was a pretty good student. He earned Bs in almost every subject. He always completed his work on time and was a member of the computer science and journalism clubs. Casey had an outgoing nature, and he even served as class vice-president during his junior year. As he neared graduation, his teachers, friends, and parents began asking him what he wanted to do with the rest of his life. He always laughed and said something funny like "president of the United States," but worry secretly gnawed at him. "I know I'm a good student and have a lot of

✔ TRUE OR FALSE?

Do You Know Who You Are?

1. It is okay to be undecided about your career path.

2. Melancholic individuals are often the life of the party.

3. It's important to work at a company that matches your values.

Test yourself as you read through this chapter. The answers appear on pages 16–17.

interests," he said to himself, "but no career seems like a good match for me. What should I do?"

Does Casey's story sound familiar? If so, you've come to the right place. You may feel frustrated that after years of education, you still don't know what you want to do with the rest of your life. Don't despair! There are millions of people in the same boat as you who just need a little help matching their interests and skills with career options. So let's get started! (Note: You may already know what you want to be in life, perhaps an engineer, teacher, or diagnostic medical sonographer. If that's the case, congratulations, but you should move on to the other chapters in this book to start learning how you can get a job.)

DID YOU KNOW?

College students do not typically have to declare a major until the end of their sophomore year.

WHO AM I?

This question may seem a little scary, but all it's really asking is, What type of personality do I have? What are my interests? What are my strengths and weaknesses? What are my values? If you can honestly assess yourself, you will be more successful finding a career that is a good fit for you.

Your Personality, Interests, Strengths, and Weaknesses

Maribel was an outgoing person who loved to talk to her friends and family on the phone and via email and text messages. She enjoyed biology, the outdoors, and blogging about the importance of protecting the environment, and she even got a chance to be interviewed by the local television station about a class project that helped restore a local wetland. "It was so exciting to be on TV and tell people about all of the good we did," she said to her parents. "I just loved it!" When Maribel graduated from college with a degree in biology, she had trouble finding a job. After sending out hundreds of resumes, a research laboratory called her for an interview, and she was offered a job as a laboratory

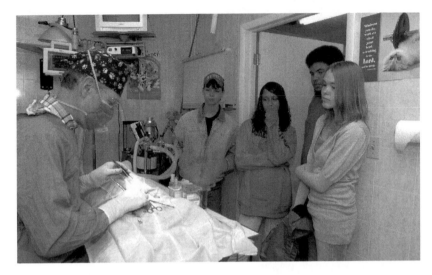

High school students participate in a career day field trip at an animal hospital. Such activities are a great way to learn about work environments and determine if your personality type and interests are a good match for a job. (Rob Morgan, Independence Daily Reporter/AP Photo)

technician. Although it wasn't quite a perfect match for her, she accepted the offer, believing that any job was better than none. After just a few weeks at work, Maribel realized she hated her job. She worked under florescent lighting in a tiny laboratory with no windows. She longed to catch a glimpse of the trees waving in the breeze and feel the sun beaming down on her face. While her coworkers were friendly, they barely spoke to one another because the work was so demanding. At times, she felt like she was in a tomb. Within a few months, Maribel had had enough, and she gave her notice.

Maribel made a critical error when choosing a career—not finding one that matched her personality type. It's important that you don't repeat Maribel's mistake.

What is your personality type? Are you outgoing, sensitive, analytical, introverted, laid-back, or a combination of these traits?

There are four main temperaments, or personality types: phlegmatic, melancholy, sanguine, and choleric. Each has corresponding strengths and weaknesses. The following paragraphs provide more information about these temperaments.

"It's important to match your personality type to a job. People with introverted and quiet personalities may have a hard time working in jobs such as sales— which require a lot of public speaking and interaction with different types of people—while those with outgoing personalities would probably thrive in such careers. Finding a job that suits your personality will make it easier to succeed in your career."

Marnie Blaylock, sales worker

Phlegmatic
Phlegmatic people are "steady-as-they-go" individuals. Their strengths are a combination of their consistency and their abilities. Those with phlegmatic personalities are easy to live with and undemand-

✍ EXERCISE

A list of personality traits for each personality type is provided on page 12. Divide a sheet of paper into four quarters. Mark one quarter with a P (for phlegmatic), one with an M (for melancholy), one with an S (for sanguine), and one with a C (for choleric). Beneath each letter, write the words or phrases from the corresponding quarters of the chart that best describe you most of the time. This will help you determine your personality type and narrow down your career choices.

ing. Phlegmatic individuals need to be sure that they don't become too laid-back and not get work done or spend too much time observing the world as it passes by. Some of the most negative traits of the phlegmatic personality are indecisiveness, laziness, and timidness.

Melancholy
Melancholic individuals are sensitive and gifted and often catch things that other people miss. They are faithful friends, willing to sacrifice for the good of others, excellent listeners, and perfectionists (which makes them dependable because they don't like to let people down). Some of the most negative traits of the melancholy personality are moodiness, shyness, and pessimism.

Sanguine

If you like being the life of the party, you might have a sanguine personality. Sanguine people enjoy trying new things and meeting new people and are seldom at a loss for words. They are typically cheerful, energetic, and good at motivating others. Some of the negative traits of the sanguine personality are arrogance, inattention to detail, and poor listening skills.

Choleric

Choleric individuals are independent and self-sufficient. They are good at making decisions and are often strong leaders. Choleric people are filled with ideas and ways to implement them. They love being in the middle of the action. These individuals need to be careful that, in their excitement at generating and implementing ideas, they don't overlook other people's needs and ideas and act like dictators. Some of the most negative traits of the choleric personality are the need to control others, argumentativeness, impatience, inflexibility, pushiness, and insensitivity.

Now that you've studied the personality types and selected traits from the Categories of Personality Traits, what do you do next? In Maribel's case, it was pretty obvious that her outgoing personality and love of the outdoors were a poor match for her job as a laboratory technician. But it may not be so easy for you to match your personality traits with an appropriate career. Luckily, there are Web sites where

CATEGORIES OF PERSONALITY TRAITS

Phlegmatic	Melancholy	Sanguine	Choleric
Easygoing	Analytical	Laughs a lot	Domineering
Discerning	Creative	Conceited	Impudent
Uninvolved	Moody	Optimistic	Logical
Not bossy	Shy	Enthusiastic	Active
Consistent	Visionary	Inspirational	Confident
Spectator	Pessimistic	Friendly	Controlled
Stubborn	Gifted	Poor listener	Poor listener
Accurate	Hypochondriac	Dislikes being alone	Enterprising
Detailed	Genius tendencies	Likes new things	Purposeful
Pleasant	Self-sacrificing	Bubbly	Hard to discourage
Submissive	Individualistic	Verbal	Determined
Rarely angry	Intense	Likes taking risks	Quarrelsome
Dry humor	Suspicious	Spontaneous	Angry
Kindhearted	Self-centered	Fun-loving	Decisive
Indecisive	Critical	Popular	Inflexible
Orderly	Fearful	Lacks follow-	Ambitious
Calm	Private	through	Goal-oriented
Adjusts well	May be depressed	Outgoing	Good planner
Reserved	Perfectionist	Pleasant	Problem solver
Steady	Emotional	Adventurous	Handles pressure
Can be lazy	Faithful friend	Initiator	well
Can imitate others	Thinks too much	Makes others laugh	Leader
Fearful	Sensitive	Likes change	Demanding
Predictable	Vengeful	Gets bored easily	Strong-willed
Laid-back	Sad	Shallow relation-	Likes a challenge
Factual	Hurt feelings	ships	Impatient
Timid	Artsy	Angry	Pushy
Sleepy	Introvert	Smiles a lot	Well-organized
Scheduled	Dependable	Visionary	Self-reliant
Peacemaker	Slow to initiate	Motivator	Opinionated
Analytical	Feels guilty	Energetic	Hot-tempered
Controlled	Solitary	Talkative	Practical
	Imaginative	Forgets easily	Independent
			Competitive
			Insensitive
			Stubborn
			Firm
			Adventurous
			Brave

you can take a personality inventory, a scientific test designed to help people pinpoint their personality types as well as their strengths and weaknesses. Visiting the following Web sites will help you match your personality and interests to a good career:

- The Career Interests Game (http:// career.missouri.edu/students/explore/ thecareerinterestsgame.php)
- The Career Key (http://www.careerkey.org)
- Holland Codes Self-Directed Search (http:// www.self-directed-search.com)
- Keirsey Temperament Sorter (http://www. keirsey.com)
- Myers-Briggs Type Indicator (http://www. myersbriggs.org)
- O*NET Online: Skills Search (http://online. onetcenter.org/skills)
- The Personality Page (http://www. personalitypage.com)
- PersonalityType.com (http://www. personalitytype.com)

YOUR VALUES

Conlan faced a tough choice. He had just been hired for an entry-level job as a public relations assistant at an electric utility company, and the hiring manager casually mentioned that the company's latest PR campaign about its green-energy initiatives was tremendously successful despite the fact that most of

SURF THE WEB: HELPFUL WEB SITES ABOUT VALUES AND ETHICS

Association for Professional and Practical Ethics
http://www.indiana.edu/~appe

Center for Ethical Business Cultures
http://www.cebcglobal.org

The Character Education Partnership
http://www.character.org

Ethics Resource Center
http://www.ethics.org

Ethics Updates
http://ethics.sandiego.edu

Institute for American Values
http://www.americanvalues.org

Institute for Global Ethics
http://www.globalethics.org

Kenan Institute for Ethics
http://kenan.ethics.duke.edu

LeaderValues.com
http://www.leader-values.com

Legalethics.com
http://legalethics.com

Poynter Online
http://www.poynter.org

The Virtues Project
http://www.virtuesproject.com

✍ **EXERCISE**

- After studying the personality types in this chapter, what would be some better job choices for Maribel?

- Which personality type do you have? What careers match your personality and interests?

its claims were "a bit of a stretch." Conlan could read between the lines and didn't like what he heard. The manager's comments suggested that Conlan would be required to falsify or "stretch" the accuracy of information to improve the company's reputation with the public. This type of activity was contrary to Conlan's values, and he decided that he would have to respectfully tell his boss that he would not be willing to lie as part of his job. Otherwise, he would have to quit his job and find one that allowed him to be more ethical.

How would you respond in this situation? Your answer will provide you with a glimpse of your values and ethics. What are values and ethics, and how are they important during the job search? Values are the things and principles that are most important to you. They involve our feelings, ideas, and beliefs. Ethics are a system of morals, a code of unwritten rules that guide how we act toward others. Strong ethics consist of fair, honest treatment of others (think of the Golden Rule).

It's very important to assess your values and ethics before you begin your job search. That way, you will be able to match your belief system (hopefully, highly ethical) to careers and companies that share these traits. For example, if an event such as the recent financial scandal on Wall Street really bothered you, you will want to avoid applying for a job at companies that have a reputation for poor ethics and questionable business practices. Otherwise, you might find yourself like Conlan, who was stuck in a situation that conflicted with his values.

✔ TRUE OR FALSE: ANSWERS

Do You Know Who You Are?

1. It is okay to be undecided about your career path.

True. Many people do not know what they want to do with their lives. Your high school and early college years are set up to help you learn about different fields. Use this time to learn about your personality type, interests, and strengths and weaknesses in order to find careers that seem like a good match.

2. Melancholic individuals are often the life of the party.

False. People with a melancholic personality are more apt to be wallflowers at a party or not even attend at all. They are often sensitive and good listeners, but they do not usually have outgoing personalities. Individuals with a sanguine personality type are the life of the party. They are cheerful and energetic, like to meet new people, and are seldom at a loss for words.

3. It's important to work at a company that matches your values.

True. If you work for a company that does not meet your moral and ethical standards, you will be unhappy and less productive.

IN SUMMARY...

- It is okay if you don't know what you want to do with your life yet. The important thing is to begin identifying your type of personality and your interests and match them with a career.

- There are four temperaments, or personality types: phlegmatic, melancholy, sanguine, and choleric. Each category has a different set of personal traits—some positive, some negative. Most of us fit into one or two of these categories.

- Values and ethics are extremely important when searching for a job. It is key that you match your moral code with appropriate employers.

2

OBTAINING EXPERIENCE BEFORE YOU ENTER THE WORKPLACE

New graduates often face a catch-22 situation when applying for jobs. Employers want them to have some experience, but many people feel that the only way they can obtain that experience is by getting a job.

But did you know that you can get experience, make valuable networking connections, and try out careers by participating in internships and volunteer activities? In fact, internships are becoming an increasingly popular hiring tool for companies. Approximately 47 percent of employers surveyed by the National Association of Colleges and Employers (NACE) said that they prefer job candidates to get

✔ TRUE OR FALSE?

Do You Know How to Get Experience?

1. I won't be able to get a job because I don't have any job experience.

2. It's important to have a good attitude during an internship.

3. Volunteer positions usually pay a salary.

Test yourself as you read through this chapter. The answers appear on pages 38–39.

their experience through an internship (including cooperative education programs).

DID YOU KNOW?

Ninety-five percent of employers surveyed by NACE say that "candidate experience is a factor in hiring decisions."

WHAT ARE INTERNSHIPS?

"Internships provide short-term, practical experience for students, recent graduates, and people changing careers," according to the *Occupational Outlook Quarterly*. They last from 10 weeks to 12 months and are designed primarily for college students (although some are open to high school students and career changers). Many internships are unpaid, while some provide a stipend or academic credit. Internships provide you with an excellent way to try out a career, learn valuable job and soft skills, and build a network of contacts in your industry.

Completing an internship increases your chances of getting a job that you'll enjoy. Not only do you discover your likes and dislikes, but you enter the job market with experience that relates to your career goals.

—"Internships: Previewing a Profession," *Occupational Outlook Quarterly,* **Summer 2006**

Your experiences as an intern will vary greatly depending on your employer and whether the program is sanctioned by your college. Some interns fetch coffee and open mail, while others get hands-on experience working on a variety of critical projects. Obviously, the best type of internship is one where you receive hands-on experience—ideally in more than one department at the company. But even if you end up performing clerical duties, you should make the most of your internship by using it as an opportunity to expand your network and make future employment contacts.

BEST PLACES TO FIND INTERNSHIPS

According to the 2007 *Recruiting Benchmarks Survey* from NACE, the following venues are the best places to find internships: on-campus recruiting events, career fairs, campus career centers, and via assistance from college faculty.

HOW DO I LOCATE INTERNSHIPS?

Internships can be found throughout the world, but for your purposes, you will probably prefer to locate an internship that is near your home or school. If you are in college, your school (both your academic department and career services office) most likely has a formal internship program established with companies in your area. If possible, it's a good idea to participate in this type of program because colleges work closely with employers to ensure that you are benefiting from the internship, not just running errands for company staff or performing repetitive tasks such as data entry. Most colleges have established guidelines for interns that companies and other organizations must agree to in order to participate in the program. These include offering preliminary training to interns, conducting period-

A college student meets with her adviser to plan an internship. An internship is an excellent way to explore career options and add experience to your resume. (James Marshall, The Image Works)

ic meetings with college intern advisers and supervisors to talk about the intern's progress/learning objectives, and requiring employers to complete an evaluation form about the work of the intern at the end of the internship.

Other ways to learn about internships include cold-contacting companies, conducting research at public libraries and on the Internet (e-Scholar, http://www.studentjobs.gov/d_Internship.asp, is a great place to start if you want to intern at a government agency), making contacts at job fairs or other networking settings, or contacting professional

INTERNSHIPS LEAD TO EMPLOYMENT

Companies are increasingly using their internship programs to spotlight potential employees, according to the 2008 Experiential Education Survey from NACE. Employers surveyed by NACE reported that they extended job offers to 70 percent of their interns—an increase of 13 percent since 2001. "Nearly 90 percent of employers who use their programs to hire say they are very or extremely satisfied with their interns, and employers consistently name the internship program as one of the most effective tools they have for hiring new college graduates," says Marilyn Mackes, NACE executive director. "Employers see results with these programs."

associations. Additionally, many large companies have formal internship programs that help identify and develop future employees. Many of these programs offer great practical experience. For example, interns at Microsoft "are given real work with actual problems to solve... [and are] charged with enabling product teams to deliver world-class software on schedule."

HOW DO I APPLY FOR AN INTERNSHIP?

How you apply for an internship will depend largely on whether you participate in a formal program or find an internship through cold calling, at a career fair, or via another method. But once you find an opportunity, you will most likely be asked to submit an application, resume, cover letter, and personal references, among other documentation. It's a good idea to apply as early as possible because internships have become popular methods to learn about careers these days. Industry experts suggest that you begin getting your materials together around Thanksgiving if you are seeking a summer internship.

If you seem like an appealing candidate, the company or organization will ask you to participate in an interview. The interview will be a lot like a job interview. The employer asks you questions about your interests, skills, and experiences and generally tries to determine if you would be a good fit for the organization. During the interview, you should also be sure to ask questions about what the internship will entail. Ask about your job responsibilities, your work hours, and the overall goals of the internship. It's important to get everything in writing, so that you will have documentation available if the internship doesn't turn out to be all that is advertised. Overall, the entire process will go more smoothly if you participate in a formal, supervised internship.

MY INTERNSHIP'S A DUD, NOW WHAT?

Victor's internship at a robotics manufacturer was nearly over, and all he had done for the last three weeks was enter production data into a database. "If

THE QUALITIES OF A SUCCESSFUL INTERN

Participating in an internship is an excellent way to learn about a career and get your foot in the door at a company. But interns sometimes take this opportunity for granted and fail to perform effectively—the surest path to *not* landing a job. Here are a few tips that will make your internship a success:

- *Remember, no one owes you anything.* An internship is an opportunity, not a right. The company is investing its time, staff, and money to provide you with an opportunity to learn, but it is taking a risk because it has no idea how you will perform. It's up to you to take advantage of this opportunity to learn and be a positive force at the company.

- *Be on time.* This should come as no surprise. You should always be on time for class, work, or appointments. Being punctual shows

I have to look at Microsoft Excel one more day, I'm going to scream," he said to himself as he entered data. As he typed, his manager walked by, smiled, and added more print-outs to Victor's in-box. Victor was studying robotics engineering in college and

people that you are dependable and serious about learning and making a contribution.

- *Have a good attitude.* It's important to be a good listener, be able to follow instructions, work diligently at each task that is assigned, and always meet deadlines.

- *Be enthusiastic.* You may have to perform some monotonous duties at times, but with quality internships, you will eventually get a chance to help out with more demanding tasks. It's important to remain enthusiastic—whether you're stuffing envelopes or helping write and design an advertising brochure that will be mailed to millions of people across the country.

- *Go the extra mile.* Always make the extra effort to get the job done. Ask for extra work if you finish tasks early. Stay late if the company is on a tight deadline for a project—your extra effort will be noted and possibly rewarded if a full-time position opens.

was told when he interviewed for the internship that there would be some data entry, but that he would also get the opportunity to work with designers creating new "smart" robot technology. He thought about speaking up, but everyone seemed so busy. So he just kept typing away diligently and waited for the internship to be over.

Not every internship, unfortunately, provides interns with a good learning opportunity. Some companies simply use interns to perform grunt work and never give them a chance to learn new skills. Victor was in a bad situation, but he made a mistake by not speaking up. If he was participating in a college-sponsored internship, he should have spoken to his internship coordinator. No matter who sponsored the internship, Victor should have taken the issue to someone in authority. So what can do you if your internship is a dud? Beyond talking to your supervisor or internship coordinator, you should:

- Consider it a trial run if the issue can't be fixed. Complete the assigned tasks, and try to maintain a positive attitude.

- Try to make the most out of the internship. Use this time at the company or organization to observe the office culture, the different management styles of workers, and the variety of ways your coworkers communicate and solve problems. This will provide you with invaluable experience and help you to be successful when you do land a job.

- Continue to try to build your network. Try to make valuable contacts with people at the company. If your manager is unwilling to help, introduce yourself to other managers or your coworkers.

THE TYPES OF INTERNSHIP PROGRAMS

There are several types of internships, according to WetFeet.com, a career resource Web site. They include cooperative education, externships, practicums, service learning, field experience, and apprenticeships.

Cooperative Education

This is the most common type of internship. Students participate in a formal program that has been created as a partnership between the college and a company. You will get the opportunity to work in fields that match your major and often receive college credit for your experiences.

Externships

Externships are a lot like job shadowing, and they last only one to three weeks. They are most popular in the legal and medical fields and are unpaid. According to WetFeet, externships "enable you to

SALARIES FOR INTERNS

In addition to the valuable experience they receive, some interns earn an hourly wage. The average hourly wage for undergraduate interns was $16.33 in 2008, according to NACE's 2008 *Experiential Education Survey*. Interns at the master's level received $25 an hour.

investigate a career field without making a long-term commitment." If you participate in an externship, you will follow a worker during a typical day on the job. You will get to learn about the worker's job duties and work environment, the pros and cons of his or her job, and the skills that are needed to be successful in that type of career.

Practicum

In a practicum, you get the opportunity to apply what you are learning in college to a real-world project. These group or individual projects are organized by your academic adviser or department head to help you get real-world experience in a field and develop relationships with potential employers.

Service Learning

Service learning is a community-based form of internship in which you develop a project that improves your community. This might involve working at a homeless shelter, assisting in a literacy program at a local high school, cleaning up a park, or helping elderly people get to medical appointments. Service-learning projects typically consist of three steps. First, you work with your adviser to establish the goals and time duration of your endeavor. Then you actually perform the work. Finally, you study your experiences and present conclusions about the effectiveness of your work.

Field Experience

Participating in fieldwork is an excellent way for people pursuing careers in science, anthropology, sociology, or other fields to gain hands-on experience. It is a good way to apply all the theory you learn in class to real-world situations. Field experiences can vary greatly based on your major and school. For example, anthropology students at Saint Louis University recently participated in fieldwork that studied the social behavior and ecology of the mantled howler monkey in Nicaragua and Costa Rica. Elementary-education students at Humboldt State University observed and participated in social studies and science classes at local elementary schools. Students in Misericordia University's Occupational Therapy Fieldwork Program received the opportunity "to apply academically acquired knowledge in assessing, planning, and implementing occupational therapy intervention programs for consumers in a wide variety of traditional and non-traditional service settings."

Apprenticeships

Participating in an apprenticeship will help you to learn a high-skilled trade such as plumbing technology, clothing design, or electronics technology. Apprenticeships usually combine both in-school education and practical experience. They offer wages that increase as you gain more experience. Apprenticeships can last anywhere from one to five years. Visit http://www.dol.gov/dol/topic/training/apprenticeship.htm for more information on apprenticeships.

DID YOU KNOW?

Internships are not just held in the summer; 61 percent of employers surveyed by the college job-search site Cbcampus.com in 2007 said they planned to hire college students or recent graduates as interns in the fall.

IT'S AN EXPERIENCE!

Recent graduates may worry that they don't have enough experience to list on their resumes. But according to NACE, "experience is not limited to paid employment." It advises job seekers to include

SURF THE WEB: INTERNSHIPS

About.com: Finding an Internship
http://jobsearch.about.com/od/
internshipssummerjobs/a/findinternship.htm

CollegeGrad.com: Internships
http://www.collegegrad.com/internships

Cooperative Education and Internship Association
http://www.ceiainc.org

University of Dreams
http://www.summerinternships.com

WetFeet
http://www.wetfeet.com/Undergrad/Internships.
aspx

on their resume any activities or accomplishments
that demonstrate their skills and abilities. These
include:

- Internships
- Part-time employment
- Work study
- Study in a foreign country
- Service learning

- Undergraduate research
- Student activities
- Professional organizations or special interest groups
- Greek organizations
- Community service/volunteer work
- Athletics or club sports
- Choir or band
- Student newspaper or radio
- Student government
- Resident assistants
- Admissions ambassadors
- Orientation leaders
- Tutoring
- Theater
- Honor societies
- Homecoming planning committee

VOLUNTEER OPPORTUNITIES

If you have trouble landing an internship, you should try to volunteer at a company or organization where you might want to work after graduation. Approximately 3.3 million college students volunteered in 2005, according to *College Students Helping America,* a report from the Corporation

A volunteer at a community center helps children with their homework. If you can't land an internship, volunteering is one of your next best options to gain experience. (David M. Grossman, The Image Works)

for National and Community Service. This is an increase of 600,000 people from 2002. Volunteering is more informal than an internship, although you will be asked to commit to working a certain number of days or hours per week. You will not receive a salary or academic credit for this work. Nearly every company or organization can use volunteers, so it will probably be much easier to land a volunteer position than an internship. Here are a few Web sites that will provide more information on volunteering:

- Corporation for National and Community Service (http://www.cns.gov)
- Volunteering in America (http://www.volunteeringinamerica.gov)
- VolunteerMatch (http://www.volunteermatch.org)

DID YOU KNOW?

Information on volunteer opportunities with federal environmental agencies—including the Bureau of Land Management, Bureau of Reclamation, Fish & Wildlife Service, Forest Service, National Park Service, Natural Resources Conservation Service, U.S. Army Corps of Engineers, and U.S. Geological Survey—can be found at http://www.volunteer.gov/gov.

✍ EXERCISE

Ask your friends or family if they have ever participated in a cooperative education opportunity, externship, practicum, service learning experience, field experience, or apprenticeship to help you understand which internship learning experience might be the best fit for you.

READ MORE ABOUT IT: INTERNSHIPS AND VOLUNTEERING

Blaustein, Arthur I. *Make a Difference: America's Guide to Volunteering and Community Service.* Rev. ed. San Francisco: Jossey-Bass, 2003.

Fedorko, Jamie, and Dwight Allott. *The Intern Files: How to Get, Keep, and Make the Most of Your Internship.* New York: Simon Spotlight Entertainment, 2006.

Gay, Kathlyn. *Volunteering: The Ultimate Teen Guide.* Lanham, Md.: The Scarecrow Press, 2007.

Liang, Jengyee. *Hello Real World! A Student's Approach To Great Internships Co-Ops and Entry Level Positions.* Charleston, S.C.: BookSurge, 2006.

Oldman, Mark. *Vault Guide to Top Internships, 2008 Edition.* Rev. ed. New York: Vault Inc., 2008.

Peterson, Robert R. *Landing the Internship or Full-Time Job During College.* Bloomington, Ind.: iUniverse Inc., 2005.

Princeton Review. *The Internship Bible.* 10th ed. New York: Princeton Review, 2004.

Rosenberg, Bob, and Guy Lampard. *Giving from Your Heart: A Guide to Volunteering.* Bloomington, Ind.: iUniverse Inc., 2005.

✔ TRUE OR FALSE: ANSWERS

Do You Know How to Get Experience?

1. I won't be able to get a job because I don't have any job experience.

False. You don't need job experience to get a job. You may not have a lot of job experience, but you have participated in all types of activities such as internships, work study, service learning, student government, and the student newspaper or radio station. While most of these activities (except for internships) do not offer pay, they do demonstrate your skills and abilities and should be placed on your resume.

2. It's important to have a good attitude during an internship.

True. An internship is a privilege, and you need to show your company that it made a good decision when it picked you. You should be enthusiastic and friendly at all times, and always be willing to take on extra tasks or stay late to help with a project that is on deadline. Interns that demonstrate these traits are often the ones who get hired for full-time positions.

3. Volunteer positions usually pay a salary.

False. Volunteer opportunities do not pay a salary, but they provide excellent experience that you can list on your resume. And if you can't get an internship, volunteering is one of the next best options to help you gain experience.

IN SUMMARY...

- Internships provide practical experience to people who are seeking to enter a career. They are an excellent way to get your foot in the door at a company, gain experience, and build your network of contacts. Internships typically last from 10 weeks to 12 months and are designed primarily for college students. Some internships offer a salary and/or academic credit, others are unpaid.

- A quality internship provides you with the opportunity to receive hands-on experience at a company in a variety of departments rather than simply doing monotonous clerical tasks or getting coffee for staff members.

- You can find internships through programs at your college or by cold-contacting companies, conducting research at libraries and on the Internet, making contacts at job fairs or other networking settings, or by contacting professional associations.

- To apply for an internship, you typically have to submit a cover letter, resume, application, and personal references, and then participate in an interview.

- It is wise to apply for internships as early as possible, since competition is strong for the best internships.

- Successful interns realize that an internship is a privilege and opportunity, not a right. They are punctual, have a good attitude, are good listeners, are enthusiastic, and are willing to make the extra effort on the job.

- The main types of internship programs include cooperative education, externships, practicums, service learning, field experience, and apprenticeships.

- Volunteering is another way to gain job experience. Most volunteer opportunities do not offer academic credit or pay.

3

RESEARCHING CAREER OPTIONS

Mike had tried for weeks to find a job, but with no luck. He had searched newspapers and the Internet but couldn't find a career that matched his skills and educational background. "I'm exhausted," he told his friend Rashid, who had just started a new job at a hospital. "I've read every newspaper job page and surfed the Internet till my eyes almost popped out of my head. I'm about ready to give up!"

"Newspapers and the Internet...that's all you tried?," Rashid asked incredulously. "It took me months to find my job, and I attended career fairs, used my college's career services office, joined a few professional associations as a student member, and even asked some of my professors for suggestions."

"I guess I really didn't do as good of a job as I thought," responded Mike. "I think I need to go back to the drawing board."

Like Mike, many people think that the Internet and newspaper job sections are the only places to

Do You Know How to Find a Job?

1. The Internet is the best way to find a job.

2. Headhunters receive their fees whether or not you like the job they find you.

3. It's a good idea to develop a 30-second marketing pitch about yourself before you attend a job fair.

Test yourself as you read through this chapter. The answers appear on pages 53–54.

find jobs. But do you know that there is a wide variety of resources available to job seekers? The following sections detail some of the most popular methods available.

COLLEGE CAREER SERVICES OFFICES

Whether you are a current college student or a recent graduate, your college career services office can be a great resource. Counselors can provide you with information on job opportunities, career fairs, campus visits by company representatives, and internships, as well as help with your resume, cover letter, and interviewing style.

Using college career services is the most effective job-search tool, according to the National Association of Colleges and Employers (NACE) 2007 *Graduating Student Survey*. Fifty-two percent of respondents who had landed a full-time job applied for the job through a campus career center-sponsored career fair. And 41 percent of respondents found a job by posting their resumes through their career center's Web site. "Our study shows that students who actually got full-time jobs tended to use their college career center and its resources more heavily than those who skipped over the career center and went directly to the employer," says Marilyn Mackes, NACE executive director.

DID YOU KNOW?

Despite the fact that college career centers provide the most effective means of helping students get a job, they trailed two other job-search methods in popularity, according to NACE. Seventy-one percent of students who responded to NACE's 2007 *Graduating Student Survey* said that they had applied for a job by submitting their resumes directly at an employer's Web site, and 47 percent mailed them directly to an employer. Applying at a career center job fair (44 percent) and posting a resume at a career center's Web site (34 percent) were the third and fourth most popular methods of applying for a job.

ON-CAMPUS RECRUITING

Companies of all sizes visit campuses to recruit students via one-on-one interviews, career fairs, and other methods. Companies surveyed by NACE in 2008 believe that on-campus visits are the most popular way to recruit new workers.

OTHER COLLEGE RESOURCES

In addition to career services offices and on-campus recruiting, don't forget to utilize other job-search resources on campus such as professors, internships, and volunteer opportunities. Your instructors may be able to recommend potential employers or may even be able to provide you with the names of hiring managers or department heads at top companies in your field. As mentioned in Chapter 2, internships and volunteer opportunities provide an excellent way to learn more about the field and perhaps even get your foot in the door. If you make a good impression during your internship, you will definitely be a more attractive candidate than an individual who has had no "face time" with the company. See Chapter 2 for more information on internships and other experiential opportunities.

DID YOU KNOW?

It pays to participate in internships, according to NACE's 2007 *Recruiting Benchmarks Survey*. Employers surveyed by NACE reported that they offered jobs to nearly 67 percent of their college interns, and 70 percent of these offers were accepted. Employers reported that nearly 31 percent of their new college hires in 2006 had participated in company-sponsored internship programs.

NEWSPAPER CLASSIFIEDS

The newspaper, in print and online, is a tried-and-true method of finding jobs. Most newspaper Web sites allow you to upload your resume. But don't be like Mike and rely on the newspaper as one of your only job-search tools; use it as a complementary resource as you search for jobs.

INTERNET JOB-SEARCH SITES

Internet job-search sites are some of the most popular destinations for job seekers. Most offer job listings and allow you to post your resume. Here are a few of the most popular job-search Web sites:

- CareerBuilder (http://www.careerbuilder.com)
- Career Journal (http://online.wsj.com/careers)
- Monster.com (http://www.monster.com)
- USAJOBS (http://www.usajobs.opm.gov)
- Yahoo! HotJobs (http://hotjobs.yahoo.com)

EMPLOYMENT PLACEMENT OFFICES

Placement offices provide a variety of services to help you get a job. A company that is hiring provides a list of its openings to a placement office, which then posts the listings and tries to match job seekers with the positions. Placement counselors can help you assess your abilities and skills and find a job that would be a good fit. You can also receive help with your resume and cover letter, get advice on interviewing skills, and receive general career counseling.

College career services offices (which were mentioned earlier in this chapter), government agencies, and for-profit organizations provide placement services to job seekers. Government agencies provide their services for free or for a small fee.

For-profit job placement services, often called headhunters, charge you for providing help in landing a job (in the form of a percentage of your hourly pay for a temporary job or a percentage of your first-year earnings if you land a full-time position; some headhunters charge the company rather than the new hire). Headhunters typically seek to represent workers with many years of experience; that way, it's easier for them to place workers, and they will earn a higher fee for placing the worker.

Be cautious if you use the services of a headhunter. To receive their fee, headhunters are motivated to find you a job—any job—and they receive their fee whether you like the job or not.

COMPANY WEB SITES

Sometimes it's a good idea to go straight to the source when looking for a job. If you know where you want to work—such as Microsoft, the Mayo Clinic, Boeing, or a small or mid-size family-run company in your area—you should visit the Web site of the employer to learn more about its products and services and find a listing of available positions. At many Web sites, you will be able to submit your resume directly to the hiring manager.

JOB FAIRS

Job fairs provide you with an opportunity to meet potential employers face-to-face. Fairs are typically organized by college career services offices, chambers of commerce, or employers. Participating companies typically have a booth where representatives, often those who are responsible for recruiting employees, talk to job hunters about opportunities at the company.

Job fairs are an excellent way to learn about a large number of companies in a variety of industries. They also provide you with a chance to network and make an impression—hopefully, a positive one—with the recruiter. Here are a few tips to make the job fair a success:

- *Conduct research ahead of time.* Learn as much as you can about the companies that are attending. Visit their Web sites to learn more about their products and services. Create a short list of questions to ask the recruiter about careers at the company. These actions will show the recruiter that you are a motivated job seeker and interested in the company.

- *Come prepared.* Bring your personal marketing tools—copies of your resume and business cards. Bring enough of both to hand out liberally. Also be sure to bring a small notebook and pen in case you want to take notes or jot down the names and phone numbers of people you meet.

- *Avoid dressing too casually.* Wear a business suit to the fair; it's always better to be overdressed than underdressed. Make a good impression on the recruiter by toning down your makeup and jewelry. Cover tattoos, if possible, and think twice about wearing piercings other than those in your ears. Men should be probably avoid piercings altogether.

- *Be enthusiastic.*

- *Network.* Treat everyone you meet—not just recruiters—as a potential source of job leads and information.

- *Prepare a marketing pitch.* Develop a 30-second description of your educational

background, skills, and career goals to
deliver to the recruiter.

- *Be a good listener.* Make good eye contact
  and listen attentively to what the recruiter
  has to say. Don't monopolize his or her
  time; this is not the time to conduct an
  information interview.

- *Mind your manners.* Always give a firm
  handshake and demonstrate good body
  language when meeting recruiters. Thank
  each recruiter for his or her time. If a
  conversation was particularly promising,
  follow up with a phone call, email, or note
  that thanks the recruiter for his or her
  time and reinforces your interest in the
  position.

PROFESSIONAL ASSOCIATIONS

Professional associations offer a variety of resources
for job-hunters—from membership for students and
professionals, to online job boards, to information
on internships, to mentoring opportunities. For
example, if you are interested in finding a job as an
environmental engineer, you might consider becoming a member of the Air and Waste Management
Association, the Association of Energy Engineers,
or the National Society of Professional Engineers,
among other organizations. If you want to become
a hydrogeologist, you might try to take advantage

SURF THE WEB: JOB FAIRS

About.com: Job Fairs
http://jobsearch.about.com/od/
jobfairs/a/jobfairs.htm

CollegeGrad.com: Job Fair Success
http://www.collegegrad.com/jobsearch/
Job-Fair-Success

eJobFairs.net
http://www.ejobfairs.net

EmploymentGuide.com: Job Fairs
http://www.employmentguide.com/
browse_jobfairs.html

QuintCareers.com: The Ten Keys to Success
at Job and Career Fairs
http://www.quintcareers.com/job_
career_fairs.html

Women for Hire
http://www.womenforhire.com

of the National Ground Water Association's Career Mentoring Database, which will link you to experienced professionals who have offered to provide career advice to aspiring ground water professionals. You might also visit the Web sites of these and other environmental associations to learn more about internships and to access job listings.

How do you find professional associations in your field? Your career services office should be able to help you locate associations, but here are a few Web sites that list professional associations:

- Association Job Boards (http://www. associationjobboards.com/find.cfm)

- International Directory of Professional Associations (http://www. associationsdirectory.org)

- *Occupational Outlook Handbook* (http://www. bls.gov/oco)

- Scholarly Societies Project (http://www.lib. uwaterloo.ca/society/overview.html)

- Weddle's Association Directory (http:// www.weddles.com/associations)

- Yahoo Directory to Professional Associations (http://dir.yahoo.com/ Business_and_Economy/Organizations/ Professional)

NETWORKING AND TAPPING THE HIDDEN JOB MARKET

The concept of networking seems complicated and time-intensive, but if you really think about it, networking is simply the process of building relationships that help you develop in your professional

✍ EXERCISE

• Create a tracking table that lists all the various type of job-search tools: college career services offices, on-campus recruiting, newspaper classifieds, Internet job-search sites, employment placement offices, company Web sites, job fairs, professional associations, networking, and the hidden job market. Use the table to ensure that you have pursued every possible option when searching for a job. Keep notes that track the methods that were most effective.

• Create a 30-second marketing pitch that details your educational background, skills, interests, and career goals.

life—from job leads and career advice to almost anything else that's job related.

The hidden job market can be defined as a collection of job openings that are available, but have not been advertised by employers. Approximately 75 to 85 percent of job openings are never advertised, so it is important that you learn the ins and outs of finding these types of jobs.

Both networking and the hidden job market will be covered in detail in Chapter 4.

✔ TRUE OR FALSE: ANSWERS

Do You Know How to Find a Job?

1. The Internet is the best way to find a job.

False. The Internet has revolutionized the job-search process because it allows job seekers to quickly reach thousands of potential employers, but there is no single best way to find a job. Other methods include college career services offices, on-campus recruiting, internships, volunteer opportunities, newspaper classifieds, employment placement offices, company Web sites, job fairs, professional associations, networking, and the hidden job market. Use the Internet AND each of these other methods to find a job.

2. Headhunters receive their fees whether or not you like the job they find you.

True. Many headhunters are ethical and highly qualified, and they will strive to find you a job that is a perfect match for your abilities. But some unethical headhunters may simply match you with any job in order to get paid. Be sure to use only reputable headhunters.

3. It's a good idea to develop a 30-second marketing pitch about yourself before you attend a job fair.

True. Recruiters and anyone else you meet at the fair will have only a finite amount of time to talk with you. That's why it's a good idea to create a brief description of yourself (including educational background, skills, and career goals) so that you can make a good impression and not monopolize anybody's time.

IN SUMMARY...

- There are many tools and resources available to help you find a job, including college career services offices, on-campus recruiting, internships, volunteer opportunities, newspaper classifieds, Internet job-search sites, employment placement offices, company Web sites, job fairs, professional associations, networking, and the hidden job market. Be sure to use all in your job search.

- Be careful when using headhunters, which are for-profit job placement agencies. They are often more interested in finding you any job—whether it's a good match for you or not—so that they can get paid (either by you or by your new employer).

- It's extremely important to come to a job fair prepared. This includes conducting research about the companies you are interested in, bringing your personal marketing tools (business cards and resumes), developing a 30-second speech that summarizes your abilities and background, dressing appropriately, and bringing a pen and paper to take notes. It's also important to be polite, listen attentively to the recruiter, be enthusiastic, demonstrate good body language and manners, and follow up promising contacts with a phone call, email, or letter.

4

NETWORKING AND TAPPING THE HIDDEN JOB MARKET

Maggie never realized that by attending her friend's birthday party she would land her first job after college. "At the party, I started talking with Mary, my friend's sister-in-law," she recalls. "She asked me what I had studied in college, and I mentioned English but lamented the difficulty I was having finding a job. Her eyes lit up, and she said, 'My friend Holly is in the publishing industry. You should talk to her. Maybe she's looking for help.' I set up an information interview with Holly, and we had a great conversation. We really clicked, and she offered me a job as an editorial assistant. Thanks to Holly and Mary—and, of course, my friend—I got a foot in the door in the publishing industry."

Maggie may not have realized it at the time, but she used networking techniques to help land a job.

✔ TRUE OR FALSE?

Are You a Good Networker? Do You Know How to Tap the Hidden Job Market?

1. Networking is conducted only face-to-face.

2. You need to dress well to be successful at a networking event.

3. E-networking is an excellent tool for those who feel that they are poor public speakers.

4. It's a good idea to apply to only the largest companies.

Test yourself as you read through this chapter. The answers appear on pages 79–80.

This may come as a surprise to people who believe that networking is complicated and time-intensive. Networking is simply the process of building quality relationships that help you obtain job leads. Networking involves reaching out and sharing and gathering information, contacts, and experiences. In traditional networking, you do this with friends, coworkers, family members, acquaintances, and even strangers in person and in writing. In e-networking, you do this online at social network sites, blogs, message boards, chat rooms, and other venues.

SURF THE WEB: JOB NETWORKING

About.com: Successful Job Search Networking
http://jobsearch.about.com/cs/networking/a/
networking.htm

Job-hunt.org: Job Clubs, Networking, and Job Search
Support by State
http://www.job-hunt.org/job-search-networking/
job-search-networking.shtml

Networking and Your Job Search: The Riley Guide
http://www.rileyguide.com/network.html

THE BASICS OF NETWORKING

You've already learned what networking is, but you probably have questions about the ins and outs of networking. The following sections provide more information.

Why Should I Network?

It will help you to get a job. Experts say that at least 60 percent of jobs are found through networking. It is a key tool to help you learn about job openings, industry trends, and a variety of other career information. You or one of your friends may have already used networking to land a summer job, internship, or other work opportunity.

When Should I Network?

Many people believe that you should wait to begin networking until you have graduated from school or lost your job. But this is too late to start using this valuable skill. While you are in school or on the job, you should constantly be reaching out to other people and building your network to learn more about job opportunities and career trends.

Where Should I Network?

There are many places to network, including formal settings such as trade and professional association meetings, career fairs, and in your office. You can also network during informal situations, such as talking with your friends, family, and neighbors; participating in social clubs, religious groups, volunteer activities, and internships and other experiential activities; and joining online social networking groups and posting messages in chat rooms or discussion groups (e-networking will be discussed later in this chapter).

How Should I Network?

Networking is basically communicating (talking, emailing, writing letters, etc.) with others. So start communicating, asking questions, and sharing information with your network. We'll provide some advice later in this chapter about what to do before, during, and after a networking event.

A recruiter (left) speaks with a job seeker at a career fair. (Jeff Greenberg, The Image Works)

MYTHS ABOUT NETWORKING

People sometimes avoid networking because they believe it is insincere. Others don't believe they can be successful because they are shy or don't have much confidence in their communication skills. If you fall victim to these misconceptions, you risk sabotaging yourself by removing a useful item from your job-search tool kit. Let's try to debunk these myths about networking.

People Who Network Are Insincere

Some people who network are insincere, but they are the least successful networkers. People who benefit most from networking are good at building genuine and honest relationships with contacts (some of which may blossom into real friendships). They give as much as they receive and are constantly looking to help others as they have been helped in the past.

I Can't Network Because I'm Shy or Lack Strong Communication Skills

It's important to remember that almost everyone is nervous when meeting new people. But everyone at networking events is in the same situation, and keeping this in mind should help you to find the courage to reach out and make new contacts. Networking is just sharing information, so if you can break down what seems like a big concept into the idea that you are just having a basic conversation (which you have every day with friends and strangers, right?), you should do fine. If you still are leery of face-to-face networking, you should focus more on networking via electronic methods including email, social networking sites such as LinkedIn and Facebook, blogs, online forums, and webcasts.

Friends, friends of friends, a barber, a neighbor, and former coworkers are often the best resources for job seekers, especially in a market with far more people out of work than job openings.

—Kelly Pate, "Everyday People Key in Job Marketing," *Denver Post*

BOOKS ABOUT NETWORKING

Bolles, Mark Emery, and Richard Nelson Bolles. *Job Hunting Online: A Guide to Using Job Listings, Message Boards, Research Sites, the Underweb, Counseling, InterNetworking Self-Assessment Tools, Niche Sites.* 5th ed. Berkeley, Calif.: Ten Speed Press, 2008.

Darling, Diane. *Networking for Career Success.* New York: McGraw-Hill, 2005.

———. *The Networking Survival Guide: Get the Success You Want By Tapping Into the People You Know.* New York: McGraw-Hill, 2003.

Hansen, Katherine. *A Foot in the Door: Networking Your Way into the Hidden Job Market.* Rev. ed. Berkeley, Calif.: Ten Speed Press, 2008.

Tullier, Michelle. *Networking for Job Search and Career Success.* 2d ed. Indianapolis, Ind.: JIST Works, 2004.

HOW TO SUCCESSFULLY NAVIGATE A NETWORKING EVENT

Tim and Natasha were just about to graduate from college with degrees in government. Both had been

TIPS FOR SUCCESSFUL NETWORKING

• Remember that networking is a two-way street. If you ask people for advice, job leads, and contacts, you need to be ready to reciprocate if asked.

• Establish a career goal or direction. Before you begin networking, make sure you have a plan of attack. People won't be able to help you if you are unable to tell them what you want (full-time job, part-time employment, etc.). If you need career direction, talk to a career counselor at your school, or ask a mentor for advice.

• Take advantage of any networking opportunities that are offered by your career center, including career days, alumni mentoring programs, and career fairs.

• Always be networking. You never know when you will meet someone who can help you. Constantly send out feelers to friends, family members, and coworkers. You can even take advantage of informal situations when you meet people at a sporting event, community meeting, grocery store, or doctor's office, or in other impromptu situations.

inspired by the recent presidential campaign and wanted to pursue a career in public service—preferably in Washington, D.C. Both were planning to go to a networking event in which representatives of the major political parties were scheduled to speak. Natasha had been planning for the event for the last week. She'd spent hours choosing an outfit, and she made sure it was cleaned, pressed, and ready to go days ahead of time. She had thought about her goals (to meet representatives of at least two public policy institutes and even a few congressional aides) and prepared her business cards. The night before the event, she stayed in to work on a short description of herself and her interests and practiced delivering it until she mastered it.

On the day of the event, Natasha woke up early and felt confident, although a little nervous. She wondered what Tim had done to prepare for the event, but he was nowhere to be found. Eventually, a friend texted her, telling her that Tim had been at a campus bar late the night before with his friends.

As Natasha affixed her name tag, she saw Tim out of the corner of her eye. Her jaw dropped. He looked like something the cat had dragged in. His hair was messy, his eyes were bloodshot, and the clothing he was wearing was completely wrinkled. He didn't even have a tie on. He was already speaking to someone, but he looked tired and disinterested. As he was concluding a conversation, she saw him fumble in his pockets looking for a business card to no avail. He simply waved his hand at the individual and walked away.

Who do you think make valuable contacts, Natasha or Tim?

Many people such as Tim believe that simply showing up is all that you need to be successful at a networking event. But did you know that there are many things you must do before, during, and after to make your experience successful? Do the following to become an expert networker:

Before the Event

1. *Define your objectives.* Ask yourself the following questions: Why am I attending? What are my goals? Am I attending to gather information about a possible career change or to actively seek a job? How many new contacts would I like to make? Is there someone in particular I would like to meet?

2. *Dress your best.* Look as professional as possible. Wear a business suit unless the event's organizer suggests business-casual dress. Make sure that every part of your look—from shoes and hair to makeup and jewelry—tells everyone you meet, "I am a professional."

3. *Prepare your business cards.* Make sure that your business cards are up to date. Bring a

sufficient number in order to be able to pass them out liberally. Bring a small notepad and pen to take notes.

During the Event

1. *Check in.*

2. *Affix your name tag.* Wear your name tag on the right side; this will allow others easy viewing when you shake hands with them.

3. *Introduce yourself effectively.* Develop a firm, but not bone-breaking, handshake. Make good eye contact. Say the following: "Hello, my name is _____. It's a pleasure to meet you." Develop a 15- to 30-second speech that describes yourself, your career, and your personal interests.

4. *Listen.* After introducing yourself, allow the other person to do the same. Participate in the conversation until it reaches its natural conclusion.

5. *Say goodbye.* When appropriate, exchange business cards. (In some situations, you may do this directly after introducing yourself.) Shake the individual's hand again and say, "It was a pleasure to meet you."

6. *Repeat.* Repeat this process until you have circulated throughout the entire room.

After the Event

1. *Follow up.* Send a written thank-you or acknowledgment to everyone you met at the event. Follow through in more detail with anybody you made a special connection with.

2. *Track your progress.* Make a chart or keep a journal of promising leads in order to follow up at a later date.

E-NETWORKING

Face-to-face meetings are not the only way to network today. Many people are using the Internet to communicate with others about careers and developments in their field. This type of networking, called e-networking, can be conducted with people you are acquainted with or those whom you've never met. Here are a few of the major types of e-networking:

Social networking sites such as Facebook are increasingly being used by people in the nursing field to search for job openings. When I was on Facebook recently, I noticed that two nurses I used to work with were looking for jobs. I knew of an open position in my department and passed this information along to them. One of them eventually landed the job.

—Vanessa Woroszylo, registered nurse

DOS AND DON'TS OF NETWORKING EVENTS

Do

- Have a game plan that details your goals
- Wear your best outfit
- Bring your business cards and paper and a pen to take notes
- Be enthusiastic
- Speak clearly and loudly enough to be heard
- Demonstrate good body language
- Observe people who network effectively, and learn from their examples
- Follow through after the event with individuals whom you've met

Don't

- Monopolize an individual's time; this will reduce both of your chances of making good contacts
- Spend the entire time linked to a friend you attended the event with; this will just deter potential contacts from approaching both of you
- Ask for a job outright because it may turn off recruiters; carefully convey your interest in learning more about job opportunities, and ask if you can contact the individual at a later time to continue your discussion.

Social Networking Sites

If you haven't heard of Facebook or LinkedIn, you've probably been shipwrecked on a desert island, or living off the grid in the wilds of Mongolia, or you're simply a Luddite (one who opposes technology). There are more than 300 social networking sites on the Internet, with MySpace (200 million users), Facebook (50 million), and LinkedIn (8 million) ranking among the most popular. What are social networking sites? Basically, they allow people to exchange information and make contacts on the web. Many operate under the "six degrees of separation" concept, in which computer software finds all the disparate connections between individuals who create a profile.

Social networking sites such as MySpace are typically more casual in nature. People use them to connect with their friends and others because of shared interests, such as a love of music or art, or shared lifetime experiences. Others, such as LinkedIn and Networking for Professionals, are geared more toward professional relationships. Some, such as Facebook, seek to exist in both worlds—business and pleasure. Here are the Web addresses for some popular social networking sites used by job seekers:

- LinkedIn (http://www.linkedin.com)
- Facebook (http://www.facebook.com)
- Networking for Professionals (http://www.networkingforprofessionals.com)
- Ryze: Business Networking (http://ryze.com)

PROS AND CONS OF E-NETWORKING

Pros

- Great for people who are not good public speakers or are shy

- Provides much faster feedback than conventional networking

- Allows you to reach a greater number of people; there are thousands of discussion groups, forums, and social networking sites available

- Allows you to network on your own time schedule

- Recruiters are "lurking" on many of these sites to search for possible job candidates

Cons

- Not as personal as conventional networking

- Keeps you from being able to use all your networking skills, such as verbal communication, body language, and the give-and-take of a face-to-face conversation

- Discussions are often not private

- You will need to provide your name and other private information to participate in many types of e-networking

DID YOU KNOW?

Almost 83 percent of college students surveyed by the National Association of Colleges and Employers in 2008 said that they had a profile on a social networking site. More than 51 percent said that expected employers to view their profile. Surprisingly, only 7.2 percent of students reported actually being contacted by an employer through a social networking site.

Web Forums and Chat Rooms

Many compare Web forums and chat rooms to conversations around the office water cooler. Information that is either informal or professional is exchanged at these Web sites. They are good places to gather information and make connections, but the quality of the information varies greatly by site.

Mailing Lists

Mailing lists have been around since the early days of the Internet and are most popular in research- and academic-oriented professions. They allow you to exchange information, including job leads, with people who share the same professional interests as you.

THE HIDDEN JOB MARKET

Tapping the hidden job market sounds mysterious—like you need to be a member of a secret employment society and have a secret password to enjoy its benefits. But it's not as complicated or scary as that. The hidden job market can be defined as a collection of job openings that are available but have not been advertised. Approximately 75 to 85 percent of job openings are never advertised, so it's important that you learn the ins and outs of finding these types of jobs.

Networking (career fairs, social networking sites, trade and professional association meetings, friends, etc.) is, of course, one of the best ways to learn about "hidden" jobs, but there are several other approaches you should use to learn about unadvertised positions. These include cold calling/emailing, information interviewing, volunteering, company Web site searches, job-hunting business cards, broadcast cover letters, and analyzing industry trends and employment projections. Each method is described briefly in the following paragraphs.

Cold Calling/Emailing

Cold calling/emailing involves contacting companies that have not placed a job advertisement to see if they are hiring. You should be prepared to face a lot of rejection, but generally speaking, most people will be civil or even friendly to you if you know a little bit about their company, learn their name ahead of time, and keep the conversation short. Even if they can't offer you a job, they might be able to recommend a company that *is* hiring.

Information Interviewing

If you happen to make a good connection when cold calling/emailing, ask the individual if you can come in for an information interview. An information interview simply involves you asking the individual about the company and career paths that match your interests. You should not expect to receive a job offer, but information is provided that can help you in your job search. But if you make a good impression, the manager may keep you in mind for future positions.

Volunteering

Take advantage of any volunteer opportunities that arise with companies in your field. By volunteering, perhaps during summer break, you'll get the opportunity to experience firsthand how a company works and find about the various career paths that are available. If you impress the volunteer coordinator, you may be considered for future positions at the company.

Company Web Site Searches

Nearly every company has at least some type of presence on the Web today. These sites can provide you with valuable information, including the types of services or products companies offer, names of key managers and other employees, and, most importantly, job openings that may not be posted on major job-search sites such as Monster or Yahoo! HotJobs.

SURF THE WEB: INFORMATION INTERVIEWING

Informational Interviewing
http://www.bls.gov/opub/ooq/2002/summer/
art03.pdf

Informational Interviewing Tutorial: A Key
Networking Tool
http://www.quintcareers.com/informational_
interviewing.html

Information Interviews Guide
http://www.career.fsu.edu/experience/
information-interviews-guide.html

Job-Hunting Business Cards

Job-hunting business cards are different from traditional business cards because they not only provide contact information, but they also provide
a link to a Web site that contains your resume,
your career portfolio (a collection of examples of a
job applicant's work and achievements) and other
information about your career. They are less intru-
sive than handing someone your complete resume
and cover letter and, because they are smaller, they
can be passed out liberally to friends and anyone
else you think might be able to help you find a
job.

Broadcast Cover Letters

Broadcast cover letters are similar to cold calling/ emailing in that you send them to companies that you are interested in but that have not advertised job openings. Why should you submit a broadcast cover letter to companies that have not expressed an interest in hiring you? According to 1st-Writer.com, you should submit a cover letter to these companies because:

- Job openings often become available without ever being posted where the public can learn about them.

- Even if there isn't a job opening, the recipient may pass your letter along to another company or division that needs someone with your qualifications and skills.

- Your cover letter may impress the recipient and encourage him or her to create a position or fire an underperforming employee.

To write a successful broadcast cover letter, you need to have good analytical skills and powers of persuasion. You need to learn as much as possible about the company (through its Web site, industry publications, etc.) and identify areas or sectors where a person of your skills and background may be needed. You then need to write a highly persuasive and detailed letter that clearly states how you would fit in at the company and how your skills would help improve its bottom line.

Analyzing Industry Trends and Employment Projections

People often make a critical mistake during the job-search process: they send resumes to large companies such as Dell, Coca-Cola, and General Electric, thinking that because these companies are so big, they must have jobs available. What job applicants don't realize is that many other people have the same idea, and these companies are inundated with resumes (often from people who lack the necessary qualifications and skills needed for success at the company).

This issue is compounded by the fact that many companies may be in the process of downsizing or may be experiencing poor sales due to changes in technology, overseas competition, or other factors. When hiring managers receive piles of resumes

TIP

Magazines such as *Forbes, Fortune,* and *BusinessWeek* publish annual guides and profiles of the best companies—including small and mid-sized firms. Visit their Web sites to learn more.

> ✍ **EXERCISE**
>
> • Create a list of people you have networked with in the past or those who you might contact in the future for help finding a job.
>
> • Learn about companies in your field by reading industry publications and visiting their Web sites.

during a time of downsizing or a poor business cycle, they often come to the conclusion that the applicants haven't done their research about the company or simply want a job whether they are qualified or not. Do you think the majority of these people will be hired? The answer is no because they have not conducted research about the company or are indifferent to market conditions that will influence hiring.

To avoid making this mistake, you need to conduct research (on the Web, via trade and business publications, at U.S. Department of Labor Web sites, and through networking) to learn which companies and industries are most likely to be hiring and which are not. You should also remember that many large companies (such as Microsoft) started out in somebody's basement or garage. It's a better idea to try to find unlisted jobs at small- to mid-sized companies that are successful and growing, rather than applying for positions at large companies that are shedding jobs.

✔ TRUE OR FALSE: ANSWERS

Are You a Good Networker? Do You Know How to Tap the Hidden Job Market?

1. Networking is conducted only face-to-face.

False. You can network in person, on the telephone, via email, and on the Internet.

2. You need to dress well to be successful at a networking event.

True. Dressing professionally sends a message to recruiters that you are competent and committed to finding a job. Visit http://career.ucsb.edu/biztech/students.html to watch a short video that offers advice on what to wear to a career fair.

3. E-networking is an excellent tool for those who feel that they are poor public speakers.

True. E-networking allows job-seekers to network without having to talk face-to-face with others. While e-networking should be an integral part of your job-search efforts, you should still learn how to become a good public speaker. Visit http://www.mindtools.com/page8.html for some tips.

4. It's a good idea to apply to only the largest companies.

False. Large companies receive thousands of resumes for a single position. A better strategy is to send your resume to small to mid-level companies in fast-growing fields such as professional and business services, health care and social assistance, education, and leisure and hospitality.

IN SUMMARY...

- Networking is the process of building quality relationships that help you obtain job leads. It is one of the key ways to find a job.

- Some of the best ways to network are through trade and professional association meetings, at career fairs, in your office, and in informal situations such as talking with your friends, family, and neighbors; participating in social clubs, religious groups, volunteer activities, and internships and other experiential activities; and joining online social networking groups and posting messages in chat rooms or discussion groups.

- It is important to begin networking as early as possible—don't wait until you lose your job or graduate from school.

- People who network successfully are sincere and treat the networking process as a two-way street. They are just as happy to provide a job lead as to receive one.

- Being shy or thinking you have poor communication skills should not deter you from networking. Remember that everyone is a little nervous talking to new people for the first time. But if you think of networking as a simple conversation, it should go a lot easier.

- E-networking consists of participating in social networking sites, Web forums and chat rooms, and mailing lists. It is much faster than conventional networking and allows you to reach a larger number of people and to network at your own pace.

- The hidden job market can be defined as a collection of job openings that are available but have not been advertised. The following methods are most popular for learning about jobs in the hidden job market: networking, cold calling/emailing, information interviewing, volunteering, company Web site searches, job-hunting business cards, broadcast cover letters, and analyzing industry trends and employment projections.

5

WRITING EFFECTIVE COVER LETTERS, RESUMES, AND CAREER PORTFOLIOS

"Learning how to write an effective cover letter was one of the best things I ever learned at my college's career services office," recalls Tiffany, an aeronautical engineer. "Before I went to one of its seminars, I thought cover letters could be two pages in length, that it didn't matter what type of paper I used, and that it wasn't important to use it to tell the employer why I deserved the job (I thought the resume would do that). Boy, did I have a lot to learn. But once I realized how important the cover letter was to my job search, I began getting more job interviews."

Writing skills are critical in your job search. Employers are looking for concise, well-written,

✔ TRUE OR FALSE?

Do You Know How to Write Winning Application Materials?

1. Cover letters aren't necessary anymore—especially because most people are submitting their resumes online.

2. It's important to use industry- and skill-friendly keywords when writing your resume.

3. It's okay to make an error or two on your resume.

4. A career portfolio should be used only by artists and fashion models.

Test yourself as you read through this chapter. The answers appear on page 110.

and visually pleasing job-search documents (such as cover letters, resumes, and career portfolios) to help them save time and quickly spotlight potential job candidates. But like Tiffany (at least early on in her job search), many job seekers lack these important skills. Eighty-one percent of employers surveyed by The Conference Board in 2006 rated high school graduates as deficient in written communication skills, so you can see that a lot of people in your age group have room for improvement. The following sections will help you hone your writing skills and create job-search documents that will make you stand out from the crowd and land a job.

TIP

Be sure to include a cover letter when you submit your resume electronically. It should be far shorter than a traditional cover letter, but still mention how you heard about the job, why you think you deserve an interview, and your achievements and skills, as well as your intention to contact the hiring manager to request an interview.

COVER LETTERS

In this age of e-resumes, you may be tempted to not include a cover letter, but this is a mistake. Cover letters, also known as application letters, are still an important part of the job search process—for both paper and online submissions. Eighty-six percent of executives surveyed by OfficeTeam, a leading staffing service, believe that cover letters are valuable when evaluating job applicants. Cover letters have five main sections: the salutation, opening paragraph, body, closing paragraph, and sign-off.

Salutation

Begin the cover letter by using the actual name of the person who is doing the hiring. Otherwise, the hiring manager may think you're lazy or not detail-oriented. If you don't know the individual's name, obtain it by visiting the company's Web site or calling the company to find out. Always use a formal salutation such as "Mr." or "Ms." To show respect for the individual, never use an individual's first name. Always double-check the spelling of the hiring manager's name.

If you're absolutely unable to locate the person's name, use "Dear hiring manager." Never use generic greetings such as "Dear sir/madam" or "To whom it may concern."

Opening Paragraph

The opening paragraph should be short and get directly to the point. List the job that you are applying for and how you learned about it. Mention contacts, if any, that you have at the company. This is also a good place to provide a synopsis of why you're a good candidate.

Body

The body of the cover letter is when you give your sales pitch—telling the hiring manager why you

TIP

When you list your contact information on your cover letter and resume, make sure that you have a professional-sounding email address, not a risqué one such as hotstuff@hotmail.com or wildman88@aol.com.

are worthy of being asked to interview. You should detail your credentials and job skills—especially those that are a good match to the ones listed in the job advertisement. You might even consider creat-

A GOOD COVER LETTER

- Has no grammatical or spelling errors
- Is addressed to an actual person at the company, not "Dear Sir or Madam"
- Conveys the personality and professionalism of the sender
- Has a friendly, but respectful, tone
- Demonstrates your knowledge of the company and industry
- Details what you can do for the company
- Is one page in length
- Is written on quality paper with appropriate fonts and point size
- Avoids clichés
- Avoids sob stories of why you should get the job
- Doesn't repeat your resume word-for-word
- Is visually attractive and has a style that matches your resume

TIP

Always re-check your cover letter template when applying to a new job to ensure that you have updated all references to a company or individual's name. You don't want to address "Mr. Smith" as "Mr. Wilson" or refer to "FedEx" when you actually mean "UPS."

ing a bulleted list of three to five of your top skills and preceding it with a statement such as "I will bring the following strengths to this position." Try to provide a short, but concrete, example of how your skills benefited your current or past employer. At some point, be sure to refer the hiring manager to your resume so that he or she will be encouraged to learn more about you.

Closing Paragraph

This is the time to issue a call for action. Don't be passive by saying "I hope to hear from you in the future." Instead, say "I will contact you shortly to see if you have received my application materials and to request a face-to-face meeting. Thank you for your time and consideration." Be sure to provide information on how and when you can be reached.

Sign-Off

Professionally end the letter by using "Sincerely," or "Best regards," and type and sign your name.

SAMPLE COVER LETTER

110001 Walden Parkway
Chicago, IL 60643
October 12, 2010

Mr. Jeffrey Jenkins
Transpo Corporation
12 Main Street
Chicago, IL 60630

Dear Mr. Jenkins:

Your advertisement for industrial engineers in the October 10 edition of the *Chicago Tribune* caught my attention. I believe that my experience with worker productivity studies, my fluency in Spanish, and my strong interpersonal and leadership skills make me an excellent candidate for the position.

I earned a bachelor's degree in industrial engineering from the University of Iowa and graduated with a 4.0 GPA. I am a student member of the Institute of Industrial Engineers. I also studied abroad in Guanajuato, Mexico, in 2008, which allowed me to become fluent in Spanish. In 2009, I participated in an internship with General Electric in which I served as a member of a team that analyzed worker productivity and usability issues as they related to the implementation of new manufacturing equipment. Because of this experience, I believe I will be able to make an immediate contribution to your company. I have enclosed my resume, which details my qualifications and provides more information on how I might be an asset to Transpo Corporation.

I will contact you shortly to see if you have received my application materials and to request a face-to-face meeting. Thank you for your time and consideration.

Sincerely,

Callie Casey

Advice on Style

Don't forget to focus on the appearance of your cover letter, not just the words and information that it contains. A visually appealing cover letter sends a message to the hiring manager that you are organized and professional. Here are a few tips to improve the look of your cover letter:

- Use a maximum of two attractive, but not overly decorative, fonts—with a point size between 10 and 12.
- Use good-quality paper.
- Use the paragraph style, although bullets may be used conservatively where appropriate.
- Mail your cover letter along with your resume in a flat business-size envelope. The second recommended style for sending your application documents is to fold them into threes with the resume on the outside.

THE RESUME

Did you know that just one typographical error on your resume could remove you from consideration for a job? Forty-seven percent of executives surveyed by OfficeTeam said that just one error would send an applicant's resume to the trash can. And 37 percent of respondents said just two errors would disqualify a candidate from consideration. That is why it is so important that you create an error-free resume. But there's a lot more to creating a winning resume than

SURF THE WEB: COVER LETTERS

About.com: Job Searching: Resumes, Cover Letters, and Employment-Related Letters
  http://jobsearch.about.com/od/resumes/u/
  resumesandletters.htm

Career Lab: Cover Letters
  http://www.careerlab.com/letters

CareerOneStop: Resumes and Interviews
  http://www.jobbankinfo.org

CollegeGrad.com: Cover Letters
  http://www.collegegrad.com/coverletters

JobStar Central: About Cover Letters
  http://www.jobstar.org/tools/resume/cletters.php

JobWeb: Resumes & Interviews
  http://www.jobweb.com/resumes_interviews.aspx

Monster Career Advice: Resume & Letters
  http://career-advice.monster.com/resume-tips/
  home.aspx

Quintessential Careers: Cover Letter Resources for Job-Seekers
  http://www.quintcareers.com/covres.html

The Riley Guide: Resumes & Cover Letters
  http://www.rileyguide.com/letters.html

Vault.com: Sample Cover Letters
  http://www.vault.com/nr/ht_list.jsp?ht_type=9

checking spelling and grammar. You need to make sure that you use the right resume format, that it effectively conveys your talents and achievements, and that it is visually pleasing, among other qualities. The following sections will help you create a successful resume.

Resumes often are a job seeker's first contact with prospective employers. Candidates who submit application materials with typographical or grammatical errors may be seen as lacking professionalism and attention to detail, and thus spoil their chances for an interview or further consideration.

—Diane Domeyer, executive director of OfficeTeam, a staffing service

THE TYPES OF RESUMES

There are several types of resume styles that you can use when applying for a job. These include the chronological, functional, combination, or targeted resume, as well a special type for recent graduates.

Chronological Resume

A chronological resume features a listing of your job experiences in reverse chronological order. Your current, or most recent, job is listed first, followed by your next most recent job, etc. This is a good resume to use if you have a strong work history.

SURF THE WEB: COVER LETTERS AND RESUMES

About.com: Job Searching: Resumes, Cover Letters, and Employment-Related Letters
http://jobsearch.about.com/od/resumes/u/resumesandletters.htm

CareerOneStop: Resumes and Interviews
http://www.jobbankinfo.org

CollegeGrad.com: Resumes
http://www.collegegrad.com/resume

JobStar Central: Resumes
http://www.jobstar.org/tools/resume

Monster Career Advice: Resumes & Letters
http://career-advice.monster.com/resume-tips/home.aspx

The Riley Guide: Resumes & Cover Letters
http://www.rileyguide.com/letters.html

Vault.com: Resumes and Advice
http://www.vault.com/index.jsp

Functional Resume

A functional resume spotlights your skills and experiences instead of your chronological work history. Employment dates are often eliminated in this type of resume. This is a good style to use if you have unexplained breaks in your work history or if you are changing jobs.

Combination Resume

A combination resume features a list of your skills and experiences followed by a chronological record of your employment history. This allows you to both spotlight particular skills that you believe will make you an attractive candidate for employment and provide a more traditional listing of your work experience. A combination resume is a good style to use if you don't have much appropriate work experience.

Targeted Resume

A targeted resume specifically lists your skills and experiences that are an exact match for the position that you are applying for. It begins with a bulleted list of these qualities followed by a chronological listing of jobs and the duties you performed at them that correspond closely to those required for the new job.

RESUMES FOR NEW HIGH SCHOOL AND COLLEGE GRADUATES

What type of resume should you prepare if you are just about to graduate or have recently graduated from high school or college? A chronological resume is not a good fit, since you do not have a long work history. A functional resume would better serve job changers and those with a gap in their employment history. Using the combination or targeted resume styles may be an option, but you still will not have a large amount of work experience to cite after listing your skills. A better idea might be to use the following format (an example is provided on pages 96–97):

1. Your name and contact information

2. Objective section (which details the position that you are seeking and the skills that you will bring to the job to help the company be successful)

3. Education section (which lists your education and achievements during college and high school)

4. Work and Internship Experience section (which lists your job and internship experiences in reverse chronological order; it will also list your achievements and, if possible, list duties or skills that are being sought by the employer)

5. Community Involvement section (which lists your volunteer activities)

6. Computer Skills section (which lists your computer and Internet skills)

7. Other Skills section (this is a good area to list any applicable skill or talent, such as language proficiency, that would not be a good fit anywhere else on the resume)

CALLIE'S RESUME

Callie Casey
110001 Walden Parkway
Chicago, IL 60643
999-234-5678 (home)
999-234-6789 (mobile)
ccasey@anywhere.com

Objective
To obtain the position of entry-level industrial engineer, in which my experience with worker productivity studies and my strong interpersonal and leadership skills can be effectively utilized to help your company increase profitability and improve productivity.

Education
University of Iowa Iowa City, Iowa, May 2010
Bachelor of Science in Industrial Engineering; Minor in Spanish
- Graduated cum laude
- President of Campus Leadership Society
- Member of Alpha Chi National Honors Society
- Studied in Guanajuato, Mexico

Walter Payton College Prep Chicago, Illinois, May 2006
- Completed Advanced Placement courses in statistics, physics, and Spanish
- Completed 40 hours of service learning that included weatherproofing 100 homes in low-income neighborhoods

Work and Internship Experience
Thomson Engineering Solutions Iowa City, Iowa, August 2006–June 2010

Office Assistant
- Recorded statistical data using Microsoft Excel
- Improved efficiency of information-processing by devising a new workflow process; the process reduced expenditures by 15 percent
- Supervised three other office assistants
- Responded to customer emails and telephone calls

General Electric Iowa City, Iowa, Fall 2009
Internship
- Analyzed worker productivity and usability issues as they related to the implementation of new manufacturing equipment

OfficeMax Chicago, Illinois, September 2004-July 2006
Store Associate
- Assistant manager of Print & Document Services Center; helped customers with their copying and other document management needs
- Named "Employee of the Month" for April 2006

Community Involvement
Habitat for Humanity Iowa City, Iowa, Summer 2010
- Collaborated with other students to help build a new house for a family that had lost its home as a result of a fire
- Served 78 hours during the summer to complete the house

Computer Skills
- Proficient with Microsoft Word, Microsoft Excel, Adobe InDesign, Adobe PhotoShop, and Internet research tools

Other Skills
- Proficient in Spanish

OTHER WAYS TO GET EXPERIENCE

"Experience is not limited to paid employment," according to the National Association of Colleges and Employers. It advises job seekers to include on their resume any activities or accomplishments that demonstrate their skills and abilities. These include:

- Internships
- Part-time employment
- Work study
- Study in a foreign country
- Service learning
- Undergraduate research
- Student activities
- Professional organizations or special interest groups
- Greek organizations
- Community service/volunteer work
- Athletics or club sports
- Choir or band
- Student newspaper or radio
- Student government
- Resident assistants
- Admissions ambassadors
- Orientation leaders
- Tutoring
- Theater
- Honor societies
- Homecoming planning committee

Playing in your school's band is one example of non-paid experience that you can list on your resume. (F. Ordonez, Syracuse Newspapers/The Image Works)

THE ELECTRONIC RESUME

Ninety-four percent of the top employers in the United States solicit electronic resumes, according to a survey by Taleo Research. They do this so that they can use scanning software to help find only the candidates who match their needs. The software looks for keywords such as "cold calling," "communication skills," or "Microsoft Office" that were listed in the job advertisement—and appear on the job applicant's resume. Do the following things to ensure that your electronic resume gets noticed by scanning software:

- Incorporate keywords listed in the job advertisement into your resume.

- Create a plain-text version of your resume that you can paste into the body of an email cover letter rather than sending it as an attachment. Many companies are leery of receiving attachments due to computer viruses, and including your resume within the body of an email will increase the chances of it being read.

- If you send your resume electronically, use a pithy subject line that will grab the reader's attention. This might include something like "Award-Winning Professional Seeking Employment" or "Reliable Multiskilled Administrative-Support Professional Seeking Employment."

The Truth, and Nothing But the Truth
It may be tempting to stretch the truth on your resume regarding your achievements or educational background. But "stretching the truth" is really just another way of saying "lying," and you don't want to do that. The news has been full of stories of company CEOs, politicians, and university presidents who have been caught misrepresenting their professional qualifications on their resumes and vitas and in other documents. They've lost their jobs and suffered public disgrace.

RESUME KEYWORDS TO AVOID

Hiring managers look at dozens—and sometimes even hundreds—of resumes to fill a single opening. Many of these resumes feature nice-sounding, but generally empty, words that fail to bring applicants' skills or accomplishments to life. In general, it is better to provide concrete examples of your workplace achievements. Show your accomplishments rather than using generic words that leave the hiring manager cold when reading your resume. CareerBuilder.com advises job applicants to avoid the following words on resumes when possible:

- Aggressive
- Ambitious
- Competent
- Creative
- Detail-oriented
- Determined
- Efficient
- Experienced
- Flexible
- Goal-oriented
- Hard-working
- Independent
- Innovative
- Knowledgeable
- Logical
- Motivated
- Meticulous
- People person
- Professional
- Reliable
- Resourceful
- Self-motivated
- Successful
- Team player
- Well-organized

TIP

There is no need to say "references available upon request" at the conclusion of your resume. It is expected that you will supply your references if asked by the employer.

Your employer won't appreciate catching you in a lie on your resume. In fact, 43 percent of hiring managers surveyed by CareerBuilder.com in 2006 said that they would "automatically dismiss a candidate" if he or she lied on a resume. So do the right thing and avoid lying on your resume.

CAREER PORTFOLIOS

Some employers want to see more than just a resume or cover letter. They want to see actual examples of a

TIP

Be sure that your resume is visually attractive. Use good-quality paper, bullet points, and an attractive—but not overly decorative—font, with a point size between 10 and 12.

A SUCCESSFUL RESUME

• Uses a style—chronological, functional, combination, or targeted—that is appropriate for your level of experience and skill set, or uses a special format for recent graduates, if appropriate

• Has no grammatical or spelling errors

• Conveys your personal skills and educational background effectively

• Details what you can do for the company

• Features keywords that match up with those listed in the job advertisement

• Is one page in length (two for professionals with many years of experience)

• Is written on quality paper with appropriate fonts and point size

• Is visually attractive and has a style that matches your cover letter

• Is kept up to date

• Does not contain lies or misrepresentations

job applicant's work. Career portfolios, according to the U.S. Department of Labor, "highlight a person's major achievements and can include awards, letters of recommendation, and examples of work." Job seekers typically present these items to the hiring manager during a job interview.

Career portfolios have typically been used by writers, teachers, photographers, engineers, models, and artists, but today they are used by job seekers from

READ MORE ABOUT IT: COVER LETTERS AND RESUMES

Beatty, Richard H. *175 High-Impact Cover Letters.* 3d ed. Hoboken, N.J.: Wiley, 2008.

Enelow, Wendy S., and Louise Kursmark. *Cover Letter Magic: Trade Secrets of Professional Resume Writers.* 3d ed. Indianapolis, Ind.: JIST Works, 2006.

Farr, Michael. *The Quick Resume & Cover Letter Book: Write and Use an Effective Resume in Only One Day.* 4th ed. Indianapolis, Ind.: JIST Works, 2007.

Greene, Brenda. *Get the Interview Every Time: Fortune 500 Hiring Professionals' Tips for Writing Winning Resumes and Cover Letters.* New York: Kaplan Business, 2004.

Ireland, Susan. *The Complete Idiot's Guide to the Perfect Resume.* 4th ed. New York: Alpha, 2006.

almost any background. Visit the following Web sites for more information on creating a career portfolio:

- Career Portfolio: Florida State University (http://www.career.fsu.edu/portfolio)

- Career Portfolio: Harrington Center for Career Development and Community Service (http://www.colby-sawyer.edu/campus-life/career/search_prep/portfolios.html)

Kennedy, Joyce Lain. *Cover Letters For Dummies.* Hoboken, N.J.: For Dummies, 2009.

———. *Resumes For Dummies.* 5th ed. Hoboken, N.J.: For Dummies, 2007.

Noble, David F. *Gallery of Best Cover Letters: Collection of Quality Cover Letters by Professional Resume Writers.* 3d ed. Indianapolis, Ind.: JIST Works, 2007.

Simons, Warren, and Rose Curtis. *The Resume.Com Guide to Writing Unbeatable Resumes.* New York: McGraw-Hill, 2004.

Wallace, Richard. *The Only Resume and Cover Letter Book You'll Ever Need: 600 Resumes for All Industries, 600 Cover Letters for Every Situation, 150 Positions from Entry Level to CEO.* Cincinnati, Ohio: Adams Media, 2008.

Yate, Martin. *Knock 'em Dead Cover Letters.* 8th ed. Cincinnati: Adams Media, 2008.

- QuintCareers.com: Proof of Performance: Career Portfolios an Emerging Trend for Both Active and Passive Job-Seekers (http://www.quintcareers.com/career_ portfolios)

Materials for a Portfolio

What type of elements do you include in a career portfolio? Here are some suggestions on appropriate materials, according to the Harrington Center for Career Development and Community Service at Colby-Sawyer College:

- Academic transcripts
- Diplomas, certificates, continuing-education units, licenses
- Course descriptions
- Test results, assessments, student appraisals, grade reports
- Honors, awards, honor society memberships
- Internships
- Apprenticeships
- Senior capstone project
- Letters of commendation and thank-you letters
- Job evaluations
- Personal Web sites or other electronic media that you have created

- Writing samples
- Workshops, conferences, seminars attended
- Independent learning activities
- Certificates/evidence of special training (military, etc.)

WHAT TO DO IF YOU'RE NOT GETTING INTERVIEWS

You excelled in college, you earned a degree in a hot field, and your resume and cover letter shine, but for some reason, you're not receiving any calls to interview. What's wrong? Ask yourself the following questions to determine if you're doing everything necessary to get an interview:

1. *Are my application materials really that great?* Advice: Double-check your cover letter and resume for spelling and grammatical errors as well as the quality of the content.

2. *Am I sending the same cover letter and resume to every company?* Advice: If so, stop! You need to customize these documents so that they are a good match for each job listing.

3. *Am I using keywords?* Advice: If not, start using them. Most large companies receive hundreds of resumes for a single position and, as a result, use scanning software to

help find only candidates who match their needs. Visit http://www.quintcareers.com/ researching_resume_keywords.html for information on keywords.

4. *Am I contacting enough employers?* Advice: Increase the number of resumes you send out to try to reach new employers in different industries where your skills would be a good match.

5. *How is my presentation at career fairs?* Advice: Revisit the way you dress, your body language and communication skills, and any other factors that may have caused you to leave a less-than-favorable impression on recruiters.

6. *Am I focusing only on the Googles and Time Warners of the world?* Advice: Expand your job search to focus on small and mid-level companies. Many large companies are laying off thousands of workers and are less likely to be hiring. It is also a fact that small and mid-level companies—especially those in fast-growing industries—hire the majority of new graduates.

7. *Am I following directions?* Advice: Are you faxing your resume when you should be mailing it? Calling a hiring manager instead of emailing as directed? If so, you are sabotaging your job search. Follow the instructions in the job ad to the letter to

ensure that you are not disqualified from consideration.

8. *Am I following up with employers?* Advice: Stay in touch with the hiring manager by following up within two weeks of sending your application materials.

9. *Am I as qualified for the position as I believe?* Advice: Reassess your fit for the job. You may be underqualified or lack computer certifications or other credentials that were requested. Use this rejection as encouragement to improve your education or earn certification—which will make you a more attractive candidate the next time you apply for a job.

✍ EXERCISE

- Find three job ads in different industries in the newspaper or online. Practice writing a unique cover letter for each position.

- Choose one job from the first exercise and create a resume. Practice your resume-writing skills by creating chronological, functional, combination, targeted, and recent graduate versions of the resume.

✔ TRUE OR FALSE: ANSWERS

Do You Know How to Write Winning Application Materials?

1. Cover letters aren't necessary anymore—especially because most people are submitting their resumes online.

False. Eighty-six percent of hiring managers believe that cover letters are still an important part of application materials—including those submitted online.

2. It's important to use industry- and skill-friendly keywords when writing your resume.

True. With the majority of companies now using resume-scanning software, it is critical that your resume and cover letter feature keywords that appear in job ads.

3. It's okay to make an error or two on your resume.

False. With competition strong for jobs, your application materials need to be perfect in every way. Otherwise, you risk having your resume tossed into the trash can.

4. A career portfolio should be used only by artists and fashion models.

False. Career portfolios can be used by anybody seeking a job.

IN SUMMARY...

- Cover letters remain a key component of your job application materials.

- A well-written cover letter and resume are integral to a successful job search.

- Cover letters have five main sections: salutation, opening paragraph, body, closing paragraph, and sign-off.

- Cover letters and resumes should be visually appealing. They should use no more than two fonts, feature a point size between 10 and 12, and be composed on high-quality paper.

- Cover letters and resumes should be mailed flat in a business-size envelope.

- A single typo on your resume or cover letter could remove you from consideration. That is why it is important to proofread your documents repeatedly until they are perfect.

- There are several types of resume styles that you can use when applying for a job, including the chronological, functional, combination, or targeted resume.

- There is also a special resume format for recent graduates. A sample can be found on pages 96–97.

- A resume for a pending or recent graduate should consist of the following sections: your name and contact information; an Objective section; an Education section; a Work and Internship Experience section; a Community Involvement section; a Computer Skills section; and an Other Skills section.

- Educational and work experiences are not the only activities you can list on your resume. You can also list internships, work study, study in a foreign country, and other activities.

- Successful electronic resumes incorporate keywords that have been listed in a job ad. Electronic resumes should be sent in the body of an email cover letter because many companies prefer not to receive email attachments—which may contain viruses.

- It is important to never lie or misrepresent your achievements in any way on your resume or cover letter.

- Career portfolios highlight an individual's major achievements and can include academic transcripts, letters of recommendation, certificates, Web sites, videos, and anything else that highlights a job seeker's accomplishments. They are now used by job applicants in many fields.

- If you are not getting interviews, you need to carefully assess every aspect of your job-search campaign—from the quality of your resume and cover letter to your performance at career fairs.

6

WHAT TO DO BEFORE, DURING, AND AFTER THE JOB INTERVIEW

Hiring managers interview an average of six candidates for each position, according to a survey of business executives at the nation's 1,000 largest companies by OfficeTeam. What does that mean for you? Strong competition. It's a tough world for job seekers right now, and what you do before, during, and after the job interview will determine whether you get the job or not. If you're well prepared, you'll hear, "Congratulations, you have the job." Fail to impress the hiring manager, and you'll hear a curt "Thank you, we'll be in touch." This chapter will provide you with the tools you need to thrive during the interview process.

✔ TRUE OR FALSE?

Are You Ready for the Job Interview?

1. It is better to be overdressed for an interview than underdressed.

2. You should never be negative in a job interview.

3. Sending a thank you note after an interview is unnecessary.

Test yourself as you read through this chapter. The answers appear on page 141.

BEFORE THE INTERVIEW

"I thought I had it all figured out," Julie says as she recalls her first interview. Now a successful executive at a manufacturing company, she can afford to look back and laugh. "But it wasn't so funny at the time," she says. "I had carefully chosen a conservative blue suit for the interview and had my hair and nails done. I even practiced my responses to possible interview questions for hours with my friend. But what I didn't do was research the company. I arrived for the interview and felt very confident. I looked professional and was easily able to answer questions about myself. But as soon as the hiring manager asked me what I knew about the company, I drew a blank. I stammered something about it being a manufacturing company, but I didn't even know what they produced (medical equipment), or that they were one of the industry leaders, or that they had an excellent mentoring program for young workers like me. In short, I blew it. The hiring manager was polite, but I knew that I had lost my chance at the job. I never made that mistake again in a job interview!"

What you do to prepare for the interview will set the tone for the entire interview process. This includes everything from researching the company, to choosing the right interview suit, to practicing how you will respond to interview questions, to getting enough sleep the night before so that you can shine during the interview. Avoid making Julie's mistake, and prepare in every possible way for the job interview.

Learn about the Company
Try to learn as much as you can about the company before you go to the interview. That way, you'll be able to answer questions such as "Do you know what types of products (or services) our company offers?" and "How do your personality and job skills reflect our company's values and mission statement?"

You can learn a lot about a company by reading industry publications, talking to current and past employees, and visiting the company's Web site, which will contain information on its mission statement, objectives, products and services, community activities, and staff. You might even find a bio or

other information on the person who will interview you—which will give you a glimpse into the
individual's personality and background. Perhaps
you might learn that the hiring manager is an avid
cyclist just like you, which is something that you
can try to work into the conversation during the
interview to break the ice.

Know Your Purpose
Anyone can go into an interview and say that he or
she will work hard, is organized, and is good at following instructions, but what employers really want
is for you to tell them what you can do for them.
This involves "selling" yourself to your employer by
detailing what skills and talents you will bring that
will help the company to do work more effectively
or quickly and earn higher revenues.

How to Look
You've probably heard the saying "don't judge a
book by its cover" but unfortunately, during an
interview, your cover (grooming and attire) will be
judged by the hiring manager. Nearly 33 percent of
employers surveyed by the National Association of
Colleges and Employers (NACE) said a candidate's
grooming would play a strong role in their opinion
of the individual. Forty-nine percent of respondents
said that a candidate's nontraditional attire would
"exert a strong influence" on their hiring decision.
"Job candidates need to remember that their over-

READ MORE ABOUT IT: DRESSING FOR SUCCESS

Henderson, Veronique, and Pat Henshaw. *Image Matters for Men: How to Dress for Success!* London: Hamlyn, 2007.

Lenius, Oscar. *A Well-Dressed Gentleman's Pocket Guide.* London: Prion, 2006.

Lerner, Dick. *Dress Like the Big Fish: How to Achieve the Image You Want and the Success You Deserve.* Omaha, Neb.: Bel Air Fashions Press, 2008.

Peres, Daniel. *Details Men's Style Manual: The Ultimate Guide for Making Your Clothes Work for You.* New York: Gotham, 2007.

Weingarten, Rachel C. *Career and Corporate Cool.* Hoboken, N.J.: Wiley, 2007.

all grooming and choice of interview attire project an image," says Marilyn Mackes, executive director of NACE. "They are marketing themselves to the employer as a potential employee, and part of marketing is the package."

You may not think how you look is important, and in a perfect world it shouldn't be. By not looking professional though, you are sabotaging your chances of landing a job. Here are some suggestions on how to dress and look for an interview:

- *Wear clean, pressed clothing.* Be sure to iron your clothes or have them dry cleaned before the interview. Check them for wear or stains, and avoid wearing shirts with frayed collars or other articles of clothing that look worn. Shine your shoes!

- *Be well groomed.* Be sure to bathe before the interview. Your hair should be professionally cut in a modern style. Men should trim their facial hair.

- *Avoid showing skin.* Save the revealing outfits for the dance club, not the interview. Wear clothing that is complimentary to your body type and covers your body appropriately.

- *Be conservative with jewelry.* Don't wear too much or excessively large jewelry. It may distract the hiring manager during the interview.

- *Tone down the piercings.* Women: Do not display more than one piercing in each ear. Men: Do not display ear piercings at all. Both sexes should steer clear of eyebrow, lip, and nose piercings. (Note: If you are applying to a more artistic or creative employer, multiple piercings—including

those in the ears, eyebrow, lip, and nose—
may be acceptable.)

- *Cover tattoos.* Some hiring managers may
  view tattoos as unprofessional. If you
  can, try to cover your tattoos so that the
  focus stays on you, not your "ink." (Note:
  Again, tattoos may be fine at more creative
  companies.)

- *Be cognizant of company culture.* Find out
  what the dress code is at the company
  before you interview. If it's a creative
  company (fashion, artistic, etc.), it may
  be okay to dress more casually. If you're
  interviewing at a conservative company or
  organization (financial, insurance-related,
  religious), you should dress accordingly.

Practice for the Interview

Another aspect of being prepared is anticipating
the questions you will be asked and how you will
respond to them. To improve your confidence,
it's a good idea to conduct a mock interview. Ask
a friend to play the role of interviewer and ask
you typical and offbeat questions to help you get
comfortable with the process and formulate your
thoughts. Some of the questions you should be
asked include:

- What would you say are your top three
  professional strengths and weaknesses?

INTERVIEW NO-NOS

- Overly tight clothing
- Flip-flops/sandals
- Athletic shoes
- Shorts
- Sweats
- Headgear
- Gum
- Food
- Heavy perfume

- What type of work environment do you prefer: quiet and private or loud and team-oriented?
- How would you describe your ideal job?
- What special skills would you bring to this position and this company?
- What are your expectations of this position? Of your manager?
- What are some things you would like to avoid in a job? In a company?
- How do your personality and job skills reflect our company's values and mission statement?

Analyze your responses, and have your friend or family member analyze them as well. Preparation should help you relax and communicate clearly when it's time for the real interview.

Prepare Questions of Your Own

It's a good idea to have some questions prepared for when you go into the interview. Hiring managers will provide you with an opportunity to ask questions about the company and your duties, and having a good list will demonstrate that you're interested in and actively pursuing the position. The answers to these questions will provide you with useful information about your job responsibilities, the company's work atmosphere, and other important topics. Here are a few suggestions:

- What will be my primary and secondary job duties?
- What are the most important skills for workers in this position?
- What is the work environment like?
- Can you tell me about the company culture?
- What sort of advancement opportunities are available?
- Will I be expected to work additional hours to complete projects?
- Is travel required for this position? If so, how much and to where?

RESOURCE

Job-interview.net (http://www.job-interview. net/Bank/JobInterviewQuestions.htm) lists more than 900 sample interview questions.

- To whom will I report? Will I manage any workers? If so, may I meet them?
- How frequently are performance reviews scheduled? How will my job performance be measured?
- Do you offer management training or mentoring programs for young workers?
- What information can you provide me regarding the stability of the company?
- What are the goals of the company in the next five years? Ten years?

DURING THE INTERVIEW

The First Ten Minutes

Hiring managers typically decide whether they will hire a candidate within 10 minutes of the start of the interview, according to a survey by Robert Half Finance & Accounting. This is remarkable because managers spend an average of 55 minutes interview-

SURF THE WEB: JOB INTERVIEWS

About.com: Job Searching: Acing the Interview
http://jobsearch.about.com/cs/interviews/a/aceinterview.htm

CareerOneStop: Resumes and Interviews
http://www.jobbankinfo.org

JobWeb: Resumes & Interviews
http://www.jobweb.com/resumes_interviews.aspx

Yahoo! HotJobs: Interviewing
http://hotjobs.yahoo.com/interview

ing staff-level applicants and 86 minutes meeting with management-level candidates. "The interview begins the moment job seekers arrive, so applicants need to project enthusiasm and confidence from the start," says Max Messmer, chairman and CEO of Robert Half International and the author of *Job Hunting For Dummies*.

This statistic tells you that you really need to impress the hiring manager in those first 10 minutes through your body language, communication skills, tone of voice, manners, and responses to his or her questions. Here are a few tips that will help you make a great first impression:

This young woman is demonstrating poor body language during a job interview. Her crossed hands and tense demeanor suggest uneasiness or shyness—traits that should be avoided during an interview. (Bob Daemmrich, The Image Works)

- Demonstrate good body language by offering a firm handshake, smiling, sitting up straight and facing the interviewer, maintaining good eye contact, and avoiding gestures such as tapping your fingers or feet, crossing your arms, or touching your face (which suggests you are nervous or have something to hide).

- Speak in a strong voice that conveys that you are confident and competent. Do not speak too quickly.

- Listen closely to what the hiring manager says. Do not interrupt.

- Say "thank you" and "please" when appropriate. Avoid using slang or other unprofessional language.

- Help break the ice by participating in small talk.

SURF THE WEB: BODY LANGUAGE

Answers.com: Body Language
   http://www.answers.com/topic/body-language

BellaOnline
   http://www.bellaonline.com/ArticlesP/art22551.asp

EffectiveCommunicating.com: Body Language for Interviews
   http://www.effective-communicating.com/body-language-for-interviews.html

Gestures: Body Language and Nonverbal Communication
   http://www.csupomona.edu/~tassi/gestures.htm#gestures

The Body of the Interview

Once you get past the first 10 minutes, you'll get into the nitty-gritty of the interview. This is the time when you will tell the interviewer about yourself and your background, answer any questions he or she may have, and have the opportunity to ask questions of your own. (Sample questions asked by hiring managers, as well as those you can ask the interviewer, are listed in the Before the Interview section of this chapter.) If you've done your research, you will be well prepared in this situation. You should continue to display the positive behaviors (such as good body language) that you exhibited during the early stages, but there are a few other things you can do to increase your chances of success, including:

- Be sure to convey your knowledge of the company's products or services, as well as how you think your skill set and background will help make you a good addition to the company.

- Don't rush through your responses. The hiring manager has allotted 30 minutes to an hour for your interview, and you should take advantage of this time to carefully present evidence (details about your skills and achievements) that supports the case for you being hired.

- Try to do something that will make you stand out. The hiring manager has probably

interviewed at least several people with
your job skills and background. At some
point, people's resumes and the interviews
can became a big blur for hiring managers.
To avoid becoming part of the blur, try to
say something that is unique that will stick
with the interviewer. Perhaps you might
comment about a photo or a personal
object on the interviewer's desk (such as a
photo from a vacation, or of the manager
running a marathon, or posed with a big
fishing catch). Participating in a little small
talk about the item—especially if you have
a common interest—will help you stand
out as an individual. You can even mention
this in your thank-you note as a means
to jog the manager's memory about your
interview.

*When we were hiring for a new editor, one candidate
stood out. Ironically, she had the least amount of
applicable work experience. She was fresh out of
school and had no editorial experience. But she had
the unique academic background we were looking for,
so she made it past the first round of interviews with
our human resources department to meet with us.
And when she interviewed with us, she handled herself
well. She made a strong, positive impression, dressed
sharply in a simple suit, and her hair and makeup were*

professional. Even though she was the youngest and least experienced applicant we met with, she projected a strong sense of confidence. I think what struck me the most was her enthusiasm—for both her area of academic expertise, and for the idea of working for our company. After speaking with her for only 10 minutes, it was clear she had a passion for what she studied, and that she really wanted to put her academic training to use by working for our company. Plus she just had an air of warmth and genuineness. All of us who interviewed her were easily able to visualize her fitting in with the rest of our department. So, even though she had the least amount of applicable work experience, she was the one we hired. We took a chance, but two years later, we know we hired the right person. All of the positive qualities we saw during her interview continue to be evident every day she comes to work. She put her heart and soul into her training sessions and diligently worked on learning everything she needed to know. She now stands out as a exemplary employee in our department.

—Janet Canny, encyclopedia editor

How to Tackle Questions From Left Field

Most interview questions cover your background, job expectations, and strengths and weaknesses. But sometimes hiring managers ask questions that seem completely out of left field. OfficeTeam asked workers to name some of the weirdest questions they've been asked during job interviews. Some of their responses include:

- "Do you have air conditioning at home?"
- "What would I find in your refrigerator?"
- "Why are manhole covers round?"
- "How will taking this job change your life?"
- "What made you move to a backward city like this one?"

There may be a method behind the hiring manager's seeming madness. "Asking a truly unexpected question will likely elicit a candid, unrehearsed response," says Liz Hughes, vice president of OfficeTeam. "As a bonus, the hiring manager will get a better sense of the person's sense of humor and ability to think quickly."

What can you do to prepare for and respond to these types of questions? OfficeTeam provides the following advice:

- *Do some research ahead of time.* Ask your friends and family if they've ever been asked strange interview questions during an interview, how they responded to them, and what they would do differently if they received a second chance to answer the question.

- *Remain calm.* Weird questions may be off-putting, but it is important to keep your cool no matter how odd the question. Look at an offbeat question as a chance to think on your feet and provide a creative answer.

- *Have a sense of humor.* A question such as "Why are manhole covers round?" might be simply an icebreaker to add a little levity to a potentially stressful situation. Show that you have a sense of humor by playing the hiring manager's game and answering the question.

Concluding an Interview

At some point during the interview, it will become clear through the hiring manager's visual and verbal cues that the interview is winding down. When this occurs, do the following:

1. Stand up and shake the hiring manager's hand and say, "Thank you for the opportunity. It was a pleasure to interview with you. I am very interested in this position, and I hope to hear from you soon."

2. If the hiring manager does not offer a time frame for the interview process, ask him or her to provide more information. You should say something like, "Can you provide me with a timeline for how long the interview process will last and when candidates can expect to hear from the company?"

3. If the hiring manager provides the information, thank him or her, shake hands again, and say goodbye.

4. If the hiring manager provides a vague
   response, ask him or her if you may call
   to inquire about the status of the position.
   Once you have the response, shake hands
   again and say goodbye.

SPECIAL INTERVIEW CONSIDERATIONS: THE SITUATIONAL INTERVIEW

In situational interviews, the hiring manager does
not ask you personal or factual questions (such as
"What is your greatest strength on the job?"), but
rather situational questions about how have or
would resolve a job challenge. This type of interview
seeks to assess your ability to think critically and
solve problems. Situational interviews are becoming more popular as employers seek to find new
ways to assess job candidates. Nearly 25 percent of
senior human-resources executives plan to use more
situational interviews in the future, according to a
survey by Novations Group, a consulting and training firm.

Some examples of situational interview questions (courtesy of the Career Services department of
George Mason University) include:

- Can you tell me about a time in which you
  had to speak up and tell other people what
  you felt or thought?

- Can you provide an example of an important goal you set and detail your progress in meeting that goal?

- Can you describe the most creative project you have completed?

- Can you tell me about a situation in the past year in which you had to deal with an angry and upset customer, classmate, or coworker?

- Can you describe the most difficult professor or supervisor you ever had, and tell me how you dealt with that individual?

SURF THE WEB: SITUATIONAL INTERVIEWS

CvTips.com: Situational Questions
    http://www.cvtips.com/interview/situational_
    questions.html

QuintCareers.com: Situational Interview Practice
Questions
    http://www.quintcareers.com/interview_
    question_database/situational.html

Situational Interviewing
    http://www.theiia.org/download.cfm?file=81429

Here are a few tips to help you prepare for situational interviews:

- Study the questions above (as well as those from the Web links on the facing page) and determine how you respond to each question.

- When composing your response, be sure to address the situation, what actions you took to address or solve the situation, and the outcome of your actions.

- Practice your responses aloud until you are confident. Each response should be from one to three minutes long.

- Keep your answers positive even if there is a legitimate reason to blame others.

- Just like traditional interview questions, ask your friends and family to quiz you with situational questions. Ideally, they should come up with new questions that will help you to learn how to think on your feet.

- Analyze your daily experiences at school and work for possible examples for use in future situational interviews.

AFTER THE INTERVIEW

Once the interview is finished, you need to complete several important tasks, including composing a brief summary of the interview, contacting your references, and sending thank-you notes.

Summarize the Interview

As soon as possible, write down the main points discussed in the interview (such as your job responsibilities, projects that you will be responsible for, salary information, name of the hiring manager or anyone else you met during the interview process,

BIGGEST JOB-SEARCH MISHAPS

OfficeTeam, a leading staffing service, asked more than 500 workers to recall "the biggest job search blunders they had heard of or witnessed." Here are a few of their responses:

- "Someone interviewed for a position and was not given the job. But he showed up anyway, saying, 'Here I am!'"

- "Someone tried to bribe me during the interview. She really wanted the job and asked how much she could pay me for it."

- "An applicant came in with his recruiter and had the recruiter answer the questions."

- "A job seeker didn't hang up the phone after calling about a job. I overheard everything he said, and it wasn't good."

- "I interviewed someone who had a jawbreaker in her mouth during the entire interview."

and other noteworthy information). If you struggled answering a particular question during the interview or it seemed like you were deficient in a certain job skill needed for the job (such as knowledge of computer software), write this down so that you can try to improve for future interviews. Some people

- "When asked what he had been doing while unemployed, the applicant said, 'Staying home and watching TV.'"
- "I interviewed a person who was only interested in the benefits and salary, and not the details and responsibilities of the job. He had a 'What's in it for me?' attitude."
- "One woman immediately described her faults to the interviewer and mentioned days she would need to take off."
- "Applicants have shown up in torn shirts, blue jeans, and flip-flops."
- "During an interview, when asked what his greatest faults were, an applicant gave too many answers. He kept going and going and going."
- "A job seeker wrote on her application, 'My boss was a jerk so I quit.'"

Source: OfficeTeam

take copious notes during the interview, but even if you did, it's still a good idea to carefully clarify and expand any information that you wrote down.

Contact Your References

Contact your references to let them know they might be contacted by the hiring manager. Give them the hiring manager's name and title and briefly provide details on the job you've interviewed for and any key topics that may be addressed. For example, the hiring manager may ask the reference about your leadership skills, your work ethic, or community service that you have performed. It's critical that you arm your reference with as much information as possible so that he or she can effectively answer any questions asked by the hiring manager. (Note: You should also send your references a note thanking them for their assistance.)

Send Thank-You Notes

On the same day as the interview, you should write and send thank-you notes to the hiring manager and anyone else who was involved in the interview process. Sending a thank-you note may help you stand out from other interviewees. "I always like to receive thank-you notes from people I have interviewed," says George Sell, a managing editor at a book publishing company. "I'm always surprised that I don't receive them from everyone who interviews. While thank-you notes alone may not get a person a job, they certainly factor in if two candidates are equally

matched and only one sends a note." Here are a
few tips that will help you write effective thank-you
notes:

- Keep notes brief and to the point. Don't
  repeat your qualifications. Instead, reiterate
  your excitement about the job and offer to
  provide any additional information that
  may be necessary.

- Type or write the note on quality paper.

- Send the thank-you note via regular mail.
  Use email only if the hiring decision is
  imminent. Sending a thank-you note via
  regular mail is more personal, and since
  hiring managers may receive hundreds
  of emails a day, a letter is less apt to be
  overlooked.

- Be confident. State: "I look forward to
  hearing from you regarding the position."

✍ EXERCISE

- Create a list of sample interview questions and
  write down how you would respond to each.

- Examine your interview outfits to check whether
  they are in good condition, are in-style, and are
  flattering to your body type. Discard any clothing
  that does not meet these standards.

This tells the hiring manager that you are confident of your abilities and expect to receive an offer.

Be Patient

After the interview, don't get worried if you don't hear from the hiring manager for a couple of weeks. The pacing of the interviewing process varies greatly by company. You may have been the first individual interviewed in what was a group of 5-10 candidates, the hiring manager may be waiting for feedback from his or her boss, or the company may just be taking its time assessing candidates. If you haven't heard from the hiring manager after two weeks, do the following:

1. Contact the hiring manager to get an update on the status of the interviewing process. See if the hiring manager is willing to provide you with a timeline, or ask if you can contact him or her in a week or two to get an update.

2. Continue to interview with other companies.

3. If you haven't heard from the hiring manager within six weeks, make one more attempt to find out about the status of the job, and then move on. Not receiving a response is a message in itself. The job may not be right for you, or the company may be having internal troubles that are out of your control.

✔ TRUE OR FALSE: ANSWERS

Are You Ready for the Job Interview?

1. It is better to be overdressed for an interview than underdressed.

True. You want to look your very best for the interview, and wearing a business suit sends a message that you have what it takes to do the job and are ready for employment.

2. You should never be negative in a job interview.

True. Avoid the temptation to criticize past employers or bosses.

3. Sending a thank you note after an interview is unnecessary.

False. Sending a thank-you note may make the difference between getting the job or not if the decision is between two equally matched candidates.

IN SUMMARY...

- Since competition is strong for jobs today, it is critical that you prepare for every aspect of the interview.

- It's a good idea to conduct as much research as possible about a company before the interview. It's also important to determine what skills and abilities you will be able to bring to an employer and to devise a way to "sell" these qualities to an employer during the interview.

- Always look your best in every way for interviews. It is better to be overdressed than underdressed.

- By practicing your responses to typical interview questions with a friend or family member, you will be able to anticipate any challenges you face during the interview. It's also important to prepare a list of questions to ask the hiring manager. This will show that you are committed to learning more about the company and provide you with valuable information about the organization.

- The first 10 minutes are critical during the job interview.

- Always demonstrate good body language, speak in a strong voice, be polite, and listen effectively during an interview.

- A situational interviews is a special type of job interview that aims to assess your ability to think critically and solve problems.

- You should do the following after an interview: summarize the interview, contact your references, and send thank-you notes to anyone involved in the interview process.

- It is okay to follow up with an employer if you haven't heard from him or her within two weeks of an interview.

7

ASSESSING
A JOB OFFER

Keisha was so excited. She'd just landed her first job at a prestigious accounting firm. She couldn't wait to see her friend Imad and tell him the good news.

"That's great!," Imad said after she told him she'd been hired. "How much are they going to pay you?," he asked.

"How ... much ... are they going to pay me!?" Keisha stammered, her face growing flushed. "I never thought to ask. What was I thinking?"

Like Keisha, many people become so excited about a job offer that they fail to inquire about salary, their job responsibilities, or the other features of a job. Some people may even be afraid to negotiate for a higher salary, believing the process will be too stressful. Others are just happy to have a job and feel that they should accept any offer they receive.

It's a major mistake not to carefully assess every aspect of your job offer—from job responsibilities

✔ TRUE OR FALSE?

Do You Know How to Assess a Job Offer?

1. Savvy job-seekers know exactly what they want from a job before they interview.

2. Salary should be discussed as early as possible during a job interview.

3. It's important to consider the quality of fringe benefits when assessing a job offer.

Test yourself as you read through this chapter. The answers appear on pages 156–157.

to salary and fringe benefits. If you fail to do this, you may be missing out on hundreds of thousands of dollars over the course of your career and find yourself working at a job that you don't like and that doesn't fit your skills and interests.

KNOW YOURSELF

Hopefully, at this point in your life, you know yourself. You've graduated from school; participated in internships, volunteer activities, information interviews, and job-shadowing programs; worked at least a few part-time or summer jobs; assessed your strengths and weaknesses; and analyzed your job and soft skills for resumes and cover letters. You know what types of skills you have and what your interests are (such as public speaking, writing computer software, solving problems using mathematics, helping others, or conducting research).

Focusing your life solely on making a buck shows a certain poverty of ambition. It asks too little of yourself. Because it's only when you hitch your wagon to something larger than yourself that you realize your true potential.

—Barack Obama, 44th President of the United States

This knowledge should stay with you during the job-search process—especially when you receive a job offer. It should tell you instantly if the job is a good fit for you or not. You may be tempted to take a job that offers a high salary but seems like a poor match for your job skills and interests. Don't do it! The extra money won't make up for the fact that you'll be miserable on the job. Here are a few questions to help you determine if you are a good fit for a job:

- What are my responsibilities? Do I have the necessary skills to do a good job?
- What are the work hours?
- Will I be required to travel for the job? If so, how often and for how long?
- Will I work indoors or outdoors or both?

- Will I be required to work overtime? If so, how often, and will I be compensated for this work?
- What types of fringe benefits are offered?

WHAT ARE YOU WORTH?

Do you know what other people with your educational background and experience are paid? If not, you'll be at a major disadvantage during the hiring process. Before you interview for a job, you should conduct research to determine average starting salaries for people in your field.

The Collegiate Employment Research Institute at Michigan State University conducts an annual survey of more than 1,000 employers. In 2008-09, it found that the average starting salary for graduates with a bachelor's degree was $46,500, although the editors of the survey point out that this figure may be somewhat inflated due to the higher salaries paid to those in technical fields. For example, new graduates in a technical field such as mechanical engineering received average starting salaries of $54,400, while those with degrees in marketing received offers of $42,200.

Where can you find specific salary information for your career? You can ask your classmates who have the same major what they are being offered, look up salary information in books (although these statistics are often outdated), and gather information at association Web sites. But probably the most detailed, current salary data is available on the Internet, with many Web sites featuring salary ranges for new graduates just entering their fields. Use these Web sites to help you determine what people with your background are earning. Have this number in the back of your mind when you are interviewing as a guide to determining whether you are receiving a fair salary offer. Here are a few of the most popular salary Web sites:

- Glassdoor.com (http://www.glassdoor.com)
- JobStar Central (http://jobstar.org)
- JobWeb (http://jobweb.com)
- Nonprofit Salaries (http://www.idealist.org/en/career/salarysurvey.html)
- Payscale.com (http://www.payscale.com)
- Salary.com (http://www.salary.com)
- Salary Website (http://www.salarywebsite.com)
- U.S. Department of Labor: Salary Estimates (http://www.salarysurvey.org)

HOW TO NEGOTIATE FOR A HIGHER SALARY

Don't be afraid to negotiate for a higher salary. It is your right—as long as you do so respectfully and can make a good argument to support your request. Jack

Chapman, the author of *Negotiating Your Salary: How to Make $1,000 a Minute,* encourages new graduates to not be offended if a salary offer doesn't match their expectations. They should view the offer as a starting point for negotiation, not something (unless otherwise indicated by the hiring manager) that is written in stone. He uses the example of a batter and a pitcher in a baseball game as an analogy for the salary negotiation that takes place between hiring manager and job applicant. The pitcher (the employer) will do everything he or she possibly can to get the batter (you) to swing at a pitch (the salary offer) that is outside the strike zone (too low). Both sides realize this is just business, and no one gets angry, but both sides try to win the duel. Salary negotiation is a competition, just like the battle between a batter and a pitcher.

So what should you do and say when you receive a low salary offer? Here are some basic steps to take:

1. Pause or say "Hmmm." Never reply to a salary offer right away. By doing this, you send a message to the hiring manager that the offer may be unacceptable. This might prompt the hiring manager to offer a slightly higher figure or to offer to give you a little time to think about it.

2. If you conducted research about typical salaries ahead of time, this is the time to make a counteroffer. A smart way to prepare is to come up with three salary figures

before the interview: an ideal dollar amount (this can be presented as a goal, so that you don't scare off the hiring manager), a salary figure that you can live with, and one that causes you to turn down the job.

3. When you're ready to make a counteroffer, say the following: "I conducted some research and found that the range for this salary for someone with my educational and experience level is $_____. I believe that my skill level would place me at this top end of the salary range. Would you consider raising your offer?"

4. At this point, the hiring manager will either meet you part way or say that he or she cannot increase the offer. The ball is back in your court, and you need to decide if you'll accept the offer.

5. If you accept the offer, thank the hiring manager for his or generosity and reiterate your interest in the position and your excitement at the opportunity to work for the company.

How to Handle an Early Salary Question During an Interview

Ideally, salaries should not be discussed in a job interview until the hiring manager makes a job offer. But sometimes, hiring managers insist on addressing salary early in the interview. What do you do in this situation? You can respond in the following manner:

- You can say, "If it is okay with you, I would prefer that we wait to discuss salary until we get further along in the interview and we both feel that I would be a good match at your company."

- If this doesn't work and the hiring manager keeps asking you to provide a salary number, you should say, "I'll be happy to answer that question, but first could you please provide me with more information about the responsibilities of the job?"

- Every once in a while, you may encounter a hiring manager who simply won't take no for an answer. In that instance, you should be ready to provide a very wide salary range (for example, $30,000 to $45,000) that provides a response but doesn't back you into a corner.

- If the hiring manager still isn't satisfied, this suggests that he or she may not even have a salary figure in mind and is expecting you, and all the subsequent interviewees, to help set a range. There may be no room for negotiation; the hiring manager is going to consider only candidates who accept this low offer. At this point, you might start asking yourself, "Do I really want to work for an employer that negotiates in this manner and cares more about the bottom line than finding a quality employee?"

DON'T FORGET TO CONSIDER FRINGE BENEFITS

When considering a salary offer, don't forget to factor in the quality of your fringe benefits (such as health insurance, vacation and sick days allotted, profit-sharing plan, etc.). Some companies provide

THE SECRETS OF SALARY NEGOTIATION

Richard Nelson Bolles is the author of the popular job-search book, *What Color Is Your Parachute?* He offers the following salary negotiation tips:

- Always wait to discuss salary until a job offer is made.

- Try to avoid being the first one to mention a salary figure.

- Conduct research before the interview to determine typical salaries in your field.

excellent benefits, which might make up for what you perceive as a low salary.

☞ FACT

The National Association of Colleges and Employers (NACE) reports the following average starting salaries in fall 2007 for graduates with a bachelor's degree:

Accounting: $46,292
Business administration/management: $43,256
Chemical engineering: $59,218
Civil engineering: $48,898
Computer science: $53,051
Economics: $47,782
Electrical engineering: $55,333
English: $31,924
History: $35,092
Management information systems: $47,407
Marketing: $39,269
Mechanical engineering: $54,057
Political science/government: $35,261

Source: NACE, *Fall 2007 Salary Survey*

THE IMPORTANCE OF GIVE-AND-TAKE

When you participate in salary negotiation, it's important do so respectfully, and you must be willing

BOOKS ON SALARY NEGOTIATION

Chapman, Jack. *Negotiating Your Salary: How to Make $1,000 a Minute.* 5th ed. Berkeley, Calif.: Ten Speed Press, 2006.

DeLuca, Matthew J., and Nanette F. DeLuca. *Perfect Phrases for Negotiating Salary and Job Offers: Hundreds of Ready-to-Use Phrases to Help You Get the Best Possible Salary, Perks or Promotion.* New York: McGraw-Hill, 2006.

Krannich, Ron. *Give Me More Money! Smart Salary Negotiation Tips for Getting Paid What You're Really Worth.* Manassas Park, Va.: Impact Publications, 2008.

Wegerbauer, Maryanne. *Next-Day Salary Negotiation: Prepare Tonight to Get Your Best Pay Tomorrow (Help in a Hurry).* Indianapolis, Ind.: JIST Works, 2007.

to compromise. You are most likely not going to get everything you want. For example, you might ask for $2,000 more in salary, but your employer may offer $1,000. While it is okay to try to get as much money as you can, you need to think about the negotiation from the hiring manager's viewpoint, too. He or she may feel that you have excellent potential, but are an unproven quantity. The hiring manager may also have only a finite amount of money budgeted for

✍ EXERCISE

Think about what type of job you will be a good match for. Consider your personal traits, interests, and work preferences (location, hours, setting, etc.). Use this information when you consider a job offer.

new positions, and you may just be one of many new workers that the company plans to hire. If the offer of an additional $1,000 seems firm, and the job is a good match, you should accept the offer graciously, thanking the hiring manager for his or her willingness to negotiate. If the hiring manager is unwilling to negotiate a higher salary, accept the offer if the job is a good fit, and move on. Never carry your unhappiness with an unsuccessful salary negotiation into your new job.

✔ TRUE OR FALSE: ANSWERS

Do You Know How to Assess a Job Offer?

1. Savvy job-seekers know exactly what they want from a job before they interview.

True. It's important to know what you want from a job, including work schedule, responsibilities, and expected salary range.

2. Salary should be discussed as early as possible during a job interview.

False. You should wait to discuss salary until a firm job offer has been made.

3. It's important to consider the quality of fringe benefits when assessing a job offer.

True. Job seekers sometimes get so caught up in assessing a salary offer that they forget to consider the important value of fringe benefits such as health insurance, vacation and sick days, and profit-sharing plans.

IN SUMMARY...

- It's important to know what type of job is a good fit before you participate in an interview.

- Never take a high-paying job that doesn't seem like a good match. You will soon find out that the extra salary doesn't make up for your dissatisfaction with the job.

- Before interviewing for a position, it's important to conduct research to determine what people in your field earn.

- It is okay to negotiate for a higher salary. The key is to conduct research to help support your request, ask for a raise respectfully, and be willing to compromise with the hiring manager.

- Always consider the value of fringe benefits when assessing a salary offer.

- If your request for an increase is denied by the hiring manager, move on and avoid carrying any negative feelings caused by this decision into your new job.

8

YOU'RE HIRED! NOW WHAT?

You've been hired! Congratulations! All your hard work has paid off, but now you face a new challenge: fitting in and thriving in your new job. There are new tasks to learn, office politics to navigate, and the challenge of building a good relationship with your boss. But before you can start tackling these complicated tasks, you must meet the simple challenges of your first day and beyond—from getting to work on time and finding your desk, to remembering the names of your coworkers and learning how to use the office copier, the fax machine, and your own computer.

WHAT TO DO ON YOUR FIRST DAY (AND BEYOND)

Your first day on the job is one of the most important times in your work life. On your first day, you will make impressions—good or bad—that will be

✔ TRUE OR FALSE?

Are You Ready for Your First Day on the Job... and Beyond?

1. I will get promoted within a year of starting my first job.

2. Developing your soft skills is extremely important to your success in the workplace.

3. Every company has unwritten rules that you should learn and follow.

Test yourself as you read through this chapter. The answers appear on pages 172–173.

hard to shed no matter what you do thereafter. And if you fail to fit into your company's culture, you may even lose your job. That's why it's key to ace this first workplace test. Here are a few tips to help you thrive and prosper in your new job:

Get to Work On Time

It's important to get to work on time or earlier throughout your work career, but it's especially critical that you do this on your first day. You want to send a message to your boss that you are motivated and dependable. If necessary, practice traveling your work route ahead of time to ensure that you allow yourself enough time to get there. Build in extra time in case you are delayed by traffic (accidents or

SURF THE WEB: HELP WITH OFFICE EQUIPMENT

Expert Village: Learn Basic Computer Skills
http://www.expertvillage.com/video-series/528_
computer-filing-system-windows.htm

How Stuff Works: How Fax Machines Work
http://communication.howstuffworks.com/fax-machine4.htm

How to Use a Scanner
http://www.aarp.org/learntech/computers/howto/Articles/a2002-07-16-scan.html

road closures), weather incidents (snow, icy roads, and heavy rainstorms), or car trouble. While these are acceptable reasons for being late, you should do whatever it takes to get to your first day on the job on time. Unacceptable reasons for being late include oversleeping, stopping to pick up breakfast/coffee, not being able to get a ride, or running out of gas.

Introduce Yourself to Your Coworkers
Your boss will most likely introduce you to your coworkers, but if he or she doesn't do so, walk around the office and say hello to everyone. It's important to begin building positive relationships with your

When meeting a coworker for the first time, smile, introduce yourself, and offer a firm, but not too strong, handshake. (Bob Daemmrich, The Image Works)

coworkers as soon as possible. This will help you to avoid miscommunications, become a member of an effective team, and get more done. Be sure to treat everyone with respect—from the janitor and secretaries to middle managers and the CEO. Learn your coworkers' names and job functions as quickly as possible. Create a floor plan as a memory tool that matches their names to offices and cubicles.

Be Positive
Smile, speak in an upbeat voice, and use good body language (a firm handshake, good eye contact, etc.) when being introduced to coworkers. Carry this positive attitude into your regular work routine.

SURF THE WEB: HOW TO ACT AND PERFORM AT WORK

About.com: Workplace Survival and Success
http://careerplanning.about.com/od/
    workplacesurvival/Workplace_Survival_and_
    Success.htm

First Day on the Job
    http://www.laworks.net/Youth_Portal/YP_Forms/
    YP_FirstDay.pdf

GradView
    http://www.gradview.com/careers/etiquette.html

Work Hard

Go the extra mile for your boss and coworkers. Always volunteer for new duties and responsibilities. You will get a good reputation as someone with a can-do spirit—something that is often in short supply in the workplace.

Be a Good Listener and Learner

Listen closely as you are taught new tasks and responsibilities. Take notes, if necessary, to help you soak up every last bit of information. Try to retain as much information as possible so you don't need to ask for help again with the same task.

One way to get along well with your boss is to listen attentively when he or she explains a new task. (Push Pictures/Corbis)

We need to steer clear of this poverty of ambition, where people want to drive fancy cars and wear nice clothes and live in nice apartments, but don't want to work hard to accomplish these things. Everyone should try to realize their full potential.

—Barack Obama, 44th President
of the United States

Ask Questions

There is no such thing as a stupid question. If you don't understand something, ask your boss or coworkers for clarification. Your coworkers will appreciate the fact that you spoke up to make sure you were performing a job correctly.

NEGATIVE WORK BEHAVIORS

The Collegiate Employment Research Institute at Michigan State University conducts an annual *Recruiting Trends* survey of more than 1,000 employers. For its 2007-08 Survey, it asked employers to name challenges they faced from new hires. The top challenges (in descending order) included:

- Sense of entitlement/unrealistic expectations
- Lack of work ethic/laziness
- Loyalty/commitment issues
- Appropriate work-life balance
- Immaturity
- Lack of confidence
- Inability to understand work required
- Poor communication skills
- Need for instant gratification

Observe

Pay close attention to everything in your workplace—from the subtle clues you get about office politics, to the protocol for standard tasks, to the unwritten rules. Learn how your boss and coworkers like to communicate and who is relied upon to make the big decisions. The more you pay attention and learn, the fewer mistakes you'll make.

Dress for Success

How you dress at your job will vary greatly based on your employer. For example, if you work on the production line at a manufacturing plant, you will dress much differently than you would if you were employed as a graphic designer at an arts weekly or as an accountant at a financial firm. It's important to carefully observe the culture and match your wardrobe to this style. One thing to remember is that how you dress makes a difference in how you are perceived by your coworkers and boss, and it may even affect your potential for promotion. Ninety-three percent of managers surveyed by OfficeTeam, a staffing service, said that a worker's style of dress "influences his or her chances of earning a promotion." So if you want to get promoted and gain the respect of your coworkers, dress for success.

Another dress-related issue that you will encounter at work is the concept of "business casual." Many workers are confused by this concept. Although they welcome the opportunity to dress a little less formally on a certain day of the week (usually on Friday), they are often afraid of crossing the line. Business casual varies by company, but it can be basically defined as a more relaxed office dress code that replaces the traditional business suit with more casual attire (khaki pants, cotton shirts, etc.). The rules governing how casual workers may dress are up to the discretion of the individual business, so be sure to check with your boss or coworkers for the standards of dress at your company. The following

Web sites will provide you with more information about business-casual dress:

- About.com: Business Casual Dress Code (http://humanresources.about.com/od/ glossaryd/g/dress_code.htm)

OFFICE WARDROBE DOS AND DON'TS

Do

- Adhere to office dress codes
- Look to coworkers for wardrobe ideas
- Maintain a professional image
- Keep your clothes clean and pressed
- Replace old, worn, inappropriate, or out-of-style clothes

Don't

- Defy office dress codes just to be different
- Try to dress "sexy"
- Wear office clothes that don't fit you well
- Wear dirty, wrinkled, or stained office clothes

- Business Casual Attire (http://www.career.
  vt.edu/JOBSEARC/BusCasual.htm)
- How to Dress Business Casual—Men
  (http://www.ehow.com/how_41_dress-
  business-casual.html)
- How to Dress Business Casual—Women
  (http://www.ehow.com/how_49_dress-
  business-casual.html)

Develop Your Soft Skills

Soft skills, such as problem solving and diplomacy, are increasingly important in the workplace. Some managers believe that these skills are more important than technical skills, which can be taught in college or on the job. In fact, 67 percent of human-resources managers surveyed by OfficeTeam and the International Association of Administrative Professionals said they would rather hire an applicant who had strong soft skills but lacked good technical skills. The most in-demand soft skills cited by human-resources managers in the survey were:

1. Organization (87 percent)

2. Verbal communication (81 percent)

3. Teamwork and collaboration (78 percent)

4. Problem solving (60 percent)

5. Tact and diplomacy (59 percent)

6. Business writing (48 percent)

7. Analytical (45 percent)

It's a good idea to try to develop as many of these skills as possible in order to become a trusted member of your work team. Your bosses will notice how you address problems and interact with your coworkers and will come to rely on you to complete larger tasks and assignments. You may even earn a raise or a promotion based on your mastery of soft skills and your ability to excel in your job.

Learn the Unwritten Rules

Most companies will provide you with an employee handbook that lists rules governing employee behavior. But even the most detailed handbook won't cover the unwritten rules of the workplace— rules that are ingrained in the workplace culture but are not usually sanctioned by the management. These might include not using the executive elevator or parking in certain parking spots, refilling the coffee maker if you pour the last cup, avoiding the company president on Tuesdays (don't ask—the unwritten rules can get pretty crazy at times!), not using a particular conference room that is reserved for members of a particular department, bringing a cake to share with the office on your birthday, or knowing that if you switch the paper size from regular to legal-size in the copier, you need to return it to the previous setting when you're done. It's a good idea to learn (and follow) these rules as quickly as possible once you start your job. It will show that you respect your coworkers and the office culture.

Get Along With Your Boss

A good relationship with your boss is integral to career success and advancement. During your first week and beyond, check in occasionally with your boss for an assessment of your progress. Ask for constructive criticism; it is a good way to learn how to become a better worker. Here are a few other ways to get on your boss's good side:

- Know your boss's likes and dislikes

- Solve your boss's problems

- Avoid making unreasonable requests

- Develop a good reputation in the office

- Always keep your boss up to date on the status of projects

- Never embarrass your boss

If you're looking for more advice on getting along with your boss, visit the following Web sites for more information:

- About.com: Getting Along With Your Boss and Co-Workers (http://careerplanning. about.com/od/bosscoworkers/Getting_Along_ With_Your_Boss_and_CoWorkers.htm)

- First30Days: How to Handle a New Boss (http://www.first30days.com/starting-a-new-job/articles/how-to-handle-a-new-boss. html#)

- SeekingSuccess.com: Getting Along With Your Boss (http://www.seekingsuccess.com/ articles/art103.php)

- Yahoo! HotJobs: Getting on the Boss's Good Side (http://hotjobs.yahoo.com/career-articles-getting_on_the_boss_s_good_side-498)

Avoid Office Politics

After a few weeks on the job, you will learn that there is a lot more going on than just work. Your coworkers may be engaging in subtle power struggles to win the approval of your boss. Other workers may form cliques and may gossip about a manager they don't like or a coworker who they believe receives special treatment. They may ask you to pick a side or gather negative information about a coworker. You may even believe that by doing so, you are ingratiating yourself with your coworkers. It's important to resist the urge to participate in office politics. By doing so, you will gain a reputation as an ethical person who is a friend to all. Most importantly, you will avoid facing disciplinary action if the office politics get ugly—which they often do—and affect the productivity of the company. So do your work, avoid office politics, and leave the negativity for others.

PUTTING IT ALL TOGETHER

Are you ready for the workforce? If you can follow the instructions provided in this chapter, you will not only survive in the workplace, you will actually thrive. With the right attitude, skills, and work ethic, the sky is the limit. You may be an entry-level worker today, but a manager five years down the road, and maybe a company CEO or even the owner of a business someday. It's all up to you. Get going and start the next chapter of your life. Good luck!

✔ TRUE OR FALSE: ANSWERS

Are You Ready for Your First Day on the Job... and Beyond?

1. I will get promoted within a year of starting my first job.

False. You may get a promotion in a year, but nothing is promised. You should never feel entitled to anything at work; promotions and raises have to be earned. The first step to putting yourself into consideration for a promotion is to focus on being the best employee you can be by arriving on time, working hard, following instructions, giving the extra effort, and doing everything else that your employer asks.

2. Developing your soft skills is extremely important to your success in the workplace.

True. Companies are seeking workers with strong soft skills. They need employees who have organizational, communication, teamwork, and problem-solving skills.

3. Every company has unwritten rules that you should learn and follow.

True. Pay close attention on your first day and every day thereafter to learn the hidden rules and social structures of your office. Doing this will ingratiate you with your coworkers and help you to fit in faster.

IN SUMMARY...

- It's important to make a good impression on your first day on the job and beyond.

- Successful workers are punctual, enthusiastic, excellent listeners, eager to learn, friendly, hardworking, good at following instructions, and strong communicators.

- There is no such thing as a dumb question. Always ask for clarification if you don't understand a job process or a task, or how to use technology.

- Successful workers follow office dress codes.

- Soft skills such as organizational, communication, teamwork, and collaboration skills are extremely important for success in the workplace.

- Learning the unwritten rules of the office— such as refilling the coffee maker if you pour the last cup—will help you get along and bond with your coworkers.

- If you want to be successful in your career, you should develop a good relationship with your boss.

- It's important to avoid participating in office politics (cliques, gossip, etc.).

WEB SITES

Apprenticeships

U.S. Department of Labor: Apprenticeship
http://www.dol.gov/dol/topic/training/apprenticeship.htm

Body Language

Answers.com: Body Language
http://www.answers.com/topic/body-language

BellaOnline
http://www.bellaonline.com/ArticlesP/art22551.asp

EffectiveCommunicating.com: Body Language for Interviews
http://www.effective-communicating.com/body-language-for-interviews.html

Gestures: Body Language and Nonverbal Communication
http://www.csupomona.edu/~tassi/gestures.htm#gestures

What the Boss' Body Language Says
http://hotjobs.yahoo.com/career-articles-what_
the_boss_body_language_says-306

Bosses

First30Days: How to Handle a New Boss
http://www.first30days.com/starting-a-new-job/
articles/how-to-handle-a-new-boss.html#

SeekingSuccess.com: Getting Along with Your Boss
http://www.seekingsuccess.com/articles/art103.
php

Yahoo! HotJobs: Getting on the Boss's Good Side
http://hotjobs.yahoo.com/career-articles-get-
ting_on_the_boss_s_good_side-498

Career Assessment

The Career Interests Game
http://career.missouri.edu/students/explore/
thecareerinterestsgame.php

The Career Key
http://www.careerkey.org

Holland Codes Self-Directed Search
http://www.self-directed-search.com

Career Portfolios

Career Portfolio: Florida State University
http://www.career.fsu.edu/portfolio

Career Portfolio: Harrington Center for Career Development and Community Service http://www.colby-sawyer.edu/campus-life/career/search_prep/portfolios.html

QuintCareers.com: Proof of Performance: Career Portfolios an Emerging Trend for Both Active and Passive Job-Seekers http://www.quintcareers.com/career_portfolios

Communication Skills

Free Management Library: Communications Skills http://www.managementhelp.org/commskls/cmm_face.htm

Cover Letters

About.com: Job Searching: Resumes, Cover Letters, and Employment-Related Letters http://jobsearch.about.com/od/resumes/u/resumesandletters.htm

Career Lab: Cover Letters http://www.careerlab.com/letters

CollegeGrad.com: Cover Letters http://www.collegegrad.com/coverletters

JobStar Central: About Cover Letters http://www.jobstar.org/tools/resume/cletters.php

Monster Career Advice: Resumes & Letters http://career-advice.monster.com/resume-tips/home.aspx

Quintessential Careers: Cover Letter Resources for
Job-Seekers
http://www.quintcareers.com/covres.html

The Riley Guide: Resumes & Cover Letters
http://www.rileyguide.com/letters.html

Vault.com: Sample Cover Letters
http://www.vault.com/nr/ht_list.jsp?ht_type=9

Dress, Office

About.com: Business Casual Dress Code
http://humanresources.about.com/od/
glossaryd/g/dress_code.htm

About.com: How to Dress for Work and Interviews
http://careerplanning.about.com/cs/
dressingforwork/a/dress_success.htm

AskMen.com: Business Casual Outfits
http://www.askmen.com/fashion/trends/21_
fashion_men.html

Business Casual Attire
http://www.career.vt.edu/JOBSEARC/BusCasual.
htm

How to Dress at a Career Fair
http://career.ucsb.edu/biztech/students.html

How to Dress Business Casual—Men
http://www.ehow.com/how_41_dress-business-
casual.html

How to Dress Business Casual—Women
http://www.ehow.com/how_49_dress-business-
casual.html

wikiHow: How to Dress for Work
http://www.wikihow.com/Dress-for-Work

Yahoo! HotJobs: The Rules of Workplace Style
http://hotjobs.yahoo.com/career-articles-the_
rules_of_workplace_style-535

Ethics

Association for Professional and Practical Ethics
http://www.indiana.edu/~appe

Center for Ethical Business Cultures
http://www.cebcglobal.org

The Character Education Partnership
http://www.character.org

Ethics Resource Center
http://www.ethics.org

Ethics Updates
http://ethics.sandiego.edu

Institute for American Values
http://www.americanvalues.org

Institute for Global Ethics
http://www.globalethics.org

Kenan Institute for Ethics
http://kenan.ethics.duke.edu

LeaderValues.com
http://www.leader-values.com

Legalethics.com
http://legalethics.com

Poynter Online
http://www.poynter.org

The Virtues Project
http://www.virtuesproject.com

First Day on the Job

About.com: Workplace Survival and Success
http://careerplanning.about.com/od/workplace-survival/Workplace_Survival_and_Success.htm

First Day on the Job
http://www.laworks.net/Youth_Portal/YP_Forms/YP_FirstDay.pdf

GradView
http://www.gradview.com/careers/etiquette.html

How Stuff Works: How Fax Machines Work
http://communication.howstuffworks.com/fax-machine4.htm

How to Use a Scanner
http://www.aarp.org/learntech/computers/howto/Articles/a2002-07-16-scan.html

General

CampusCareerCenter.com
http://www.campuscareercenter.com

JobWeb.com
http://www.jobweb.com

MindTools: Essential Skills for an Excellent Career
http://www.mindtools.com

Work911.com
http://www.work911.com

O*NET OnLine
http://online.onetcenter.org

Information Interviewing

Informational Interviewing
http://www.bls.gov/opub/ooq/2002/summer/
art03.pdf

Informational Interviewing Tutorial: A Key
Networking Tool
http://www.quintcareers.com/informational_
interviewing.html

Information Interviews Guide
http://www.career.fsu.edu/experience/informa-
tion-interviews-guide.html

Internships

About.com: Finding an Internship
http://jobsearch.about.com/od/
internshipssummerjobs/a/findinternship.htm

CollegeGrad.com: Internships
http://www.collegegrad.com/internships

Cooperative Education and Internship Association
http://www.ceiainc.org

E-scholar
http://www.studentjobs.gov/d_Internship.asp

University of Dreams
http://www.summerinternships.com

WetFeet
http://www.wetfeet.com/Undergrad/Internships.
aspx

Interviewing

About.com: Job Searching: Acing the Interview
http://jobsearch.about.com/cs/interviews/a/
aceinterview.htm

CareerOneStop: Resumes and Interviews
http://www.jobbankinfo.org

Job-interview.net
http://www.job-interview.net/Bank/
JobInterviewQuestions.htm

JobWeb: Resumes & Interviews
http://www.jobweb.com/resumes_interviews.
aspx

Yahoo! HotJobs: Interviewing
http://hotjobs.yahoo.com/interview

Job Fairs

About.com: Job Fairs
http://jobsearch.about.com/od/jobfairs/a/job-
fairs.htm

CollegeGrad.com:Job Fair Success
http://www.collegegrad.com/jobsearch/Job-Fair-
Success

eJobFairs.net
http://www.ejobfairs.net

EmploymentGuide.com: Job Fairs
http://www.employmentguide.com/browse_job-
fairs.html

QuintCareers.com: The Ten Keys to Success at Job
and Career Fairs
http://www.quintcareers.com/job_career_fairs.
html

Women for Hire
http://www.womenforhire.com

Networking

About.com: Successful Job Search Networking
http://jobsearch.about.com/cs/networking/a/
networking.htm

Job-hunt.org: Job Clubs, Networking, and Job
Search Support by State
http://www.job-hunt.org/job-search-networking/
job-search-networking.shtml

Networking and Your Job Search: The Riley Guide
http://www.rileyguide.com/network.html

Office Skills

Expert Village: Learn Basic Computer Skills
http://www.expertvillage.com/video-series/528_
computer-filing-system-windows.htm

How Stuff Works: How Fax Machines Work
http://communication.howstuffworks.com/fax-
machine4.htm

How Stuff Works: How Virtual Offices Work
http://communication.howstuffworks.com/
virtual-office.htm

How to Use a Scanner
http://www.aarp.org/learntech/computers/
howto/Articles/a2002-07-16-scan.html

Personality Assessment

Keirsey Temperament Sorter
http://www.keirsey.com

Myers-Briggs Type Indicator
http://www.myersbriggs.org

The Personality Page
http://www.personalitypage.com

PersonalityType.com
http://www.personalitytype.com

Professional Associations

Association Job Boards
http://www.associationjobboards.com/find.cfm

International Directory of Professional Associations
http://www.associationsdirectory.org

Occupational Outlook Handbook
http://www.bls.gov/oco

Scholarly Societies Project
http://www.lib.uwaterloo.ca/society/overview.
html

Weddle's Association Directory
http://www.weddles.com/associations

Yahoo Directory to Professional Associations
http://dir.yahoo.com/Business_and_Economy/
Organizations/Professional

Public Speaking

MindTools: Improve Your Communication Skills
http://www.mindtools.com/page8.html

WannaLearn.com: Personal Enrichment: Public
Speaking
http://www.wannalearn.com/Personal_
Enrichment/Public_Speaking

Resumes

About.com: Job Searching: Resumes, Cover Letters,
and Employment-Related Letters
http://jobsearch.about.com/od/resumes/u/
resumesandletters.htm

CareerOneStop: Resumes and Interviews
http://www.jobbankinfo.org

CollegeGrad.com: Resumes
http://www.collegegrad.com/resume

JobStar Central: Resumes
http://www.jobstar.org/tools/resume

JobWeb: Resumes & Interviews
http://www.jobweb.com/resumes_interviews.
aspx

Monster Career Advice: Resumes & Letters
http://career-advice.monster.com/resume-tips/
home.aspx

The Riley Guide: Resumes & Cover Letters
http://www.rileyguide.com/letters.html

Vault.com: Resumes and Advice
http://www.vault.com/index.jsp

Salary

Glassdoor.com
http://www.glassdoor.com

JobStar Central
http://jobstar.org

Nonprofit Salaries
http://www.idealist.org/en/career/salarysurvey.
html

Payscale.com
http://www.payscale.com

Salary.com
http://www.salary.com

Salary Website
http://www.salarywebsite.com

U.S. Department of Labor: Salary Estimates
http://www.salarysurvey.org

Situational Interviews

CvTips.com: Situational Questions
http://www.cvtips.com/interview/situational_
questions.html

QuintCareers.com: Situational Interview Practice
 Questions
 http://www.quintcareers.com/interview_ques-
 tion_database/situational.html

Situational Interviewing
 http://www.theiia.org/download.
 cfm?file=81429

Time Management

Free Management Library: Time Management
 http://www.managementhelp.org/prsn_prd/
 time_mng.htm

MindTools.com: Time Management
 http://www.mindtools.com/pages/main/
 newMN_HTE.htm

Time Management: You Versus the Clock
 http://pbskids.org/itsmylife/school/time/index.
 html

Volunteering

Corporation for National and Community
 Service
 http://www.cns.gov

Volunteer.gov
 http://www.volunteer.gov/gov

Volunteering in America
 http://www.volunteeringinamerica.gov

VolunteerMatch
 http://www.volunteermatch.org

Women

Catalyst
http://www.catalyst.org

Women's Rights at Work
http://www.citizenactionny.org

Writing

About.com: Writing Skills
http://careerplanning.about.com/cs/miscskills/a/
writing_skills.htm

GLOSSARY

apprenticeship a combination of in-school education and practical experience that enables students to learn a high-skilled trade and earn wages that increase as they gain more experience

body language the gestures, movements, and mannerisms a person uses to intentionally or unintentionally communicate moods and opinions to others

broadcast cover letter a letter seeking employment sent to a company that has not advertised job openings; it explains persuasively and in detail your skills and background and how they would be useful to the company

business card a preprinted 2" by 3-1/2" card with your name and contact information (such as phone number and email address) on it

business casual a more relaxed office dress code that replaces the traditional business suit with more casual attire (khaki pants, cotton shirts, etc.); the rules governing how casual workers may dress are up to the discretion of the individual business

career a rewarding occupation that offers the potential for advancement and higher earnings

career portfolio a collection of examples of a job applicant's work and achievements, usually presented to a hiring manager at a job interview; may include awards received and letters of recommendation; may also be found at a Web site

casual Friday workday in which a company allows its employees to dress less formally than on other days of the week

choleric one of the four temperaments; usually confident, goal-oriented, and capable

cold calling/emailing telephoning or emailing companies that have not advertised job openings to see if they are hiring

cold cover letter an unprompted cover letter that is sent to a company that has not advertised job openings; also known as an uninvited cover letter

cooperative education a program created as a partnership between a college and a company that gives students the opportunity to work in fields that match their major and receive college credit for their experiences

cover letter also called an application letter; briefly describes your interests in a job and your qualifications

electronic resume a brief listing of your job objective, education, and job experience that is prepared specifically for forwarding to recruiters via email or for posting in online job-search databases

email electronic mail, which is sent via computer and telephone and cable lines from one person to another

e-networking using the Internet to communicate with others about careers and developments in one's field of interest

ethics a system of morals; the code of unwritten rules governing how we act toward others

externship a form of job shadowing that allows students to investigate a career field without making a long-term commitment; most popular in the legal and medical fields, they last only one to three weeks and are unpaid

field experience a way for students interested in science, anthropology, sociology, or similar fields to apply theory learned in class to real-world situations in their area of study

Golden Rule the idea that you should treat others as you want to be treated

headhunter a company or individual that charges a fee for providing help in finding a job

hidden job market a collection of job openings that have not been advertised; may make up 75 to 85 percent of available jobs

information interview a meeting with the hiring manager of a company simply to ask questions about the company and gather information about possible career paths within it

Internet the name for the vast collection of interconnected computer networks around the world

internship a temporary position with a company in a student's field of study that gives a student experience in his or her field of interest, allows him or her to make contacts within that field, and may provide school credit and/or pay

job fair a formal exhibition where job-seekers receive the opportunity to meet potential employers face-to-face; also referred to as a career fair or career expo

job-hunting business cards business cards that provide, in addition to contact information, a link to a Web site that contains one's resume and other career information

job interview a meeting with the hiring manager of a company to which you have applied for a job;

the first step in determining whether your qualifications are a good match for the company

job an occupation that does not offers much opportunity for advancement and higher earnings

letter of recommendation a letter of reference
from a former teacher, supervisor, or coworker
that summarizes your work habits and personality traits; often used to apply to a school, win a
scholarship, or get a job

melancholy one of the four temperaments; usually
artistic, organized, analytical, and sensitive

mentor a teacher, coach, or adviser

networking communicating with others to share
and gather information about job openings,
industry trends, and a variety of other career
information

nonprofit organization an organization that
provides a service (often humanitarian in nature)
and whose aim is not to make money, but to earn
enough to cover expenses and stay in operation

on-campus recruiting visiting of college campuses by companies for the purpose of recruiting
new workers; may take the form of career fairs or
one-on-one interviews

personality inventory a scientific test designed
to help people pinpoint their personality types as
well as their strengths and weaknesses

personal marketing tools copies of one's resume and business cards; to be handed out liberally at job fairs and networking events

phlegmatic one of the four temperaments; generally easygoing, well-balanced, and steady

placement office a service provider that advertises, and recruits employees to fill, job openings on behalf of a company that wants to add new workers

practicum a group or individual project organized by a college academic adviser or department head to help students apply what they are learning to a real-world project

professional association an organization of professionals in a specific field that exists to further the interests of its members; a possible source of job leads and other career information in a specific field

promotion advancement in pay or position at a company

references statements by employers and colleagues that attest to your qualities as an employee

resume a brief listing of your job objective, education, and job experience that is used to apply for employment

sanguine one of the four temperaments; usually outgoing, lively, and popular

search engine computer software used to locate specific information

service learning a community-based form of internship in which students do work that benefits their communities (such as helping at homeless shelters or with literacy programs)

social networking sites Web sites (some casual, others more professionally focused) that allow people to exchange information and make contacts on the Internet

social skills the ability to interact with others

soft skills nontechnical workplace skills such as problem solving and diplomacy

temperament one's normal frame of mind and natural disposition

unwritten rules required behavior that is expected, but not stated in any manual, meeting, etc.; rules that are expected to be followed by others in an organization or common group

values the things and principles that are most important to us

vita a comprehensive, detailed written summary of your professional background that addresses your qualifications for a job.

volunteering choosing to work without pay or academic credit for a company or organization in one's field in order to experience firsthand how the company works and find out about the various career paths that are available

work ethic a system of values in which great emphasis is placed on working hard

World Wide Web interconnected information residing on the Internet

BIBLIOGRAPHY

Andersen, Peter. *The Complete Idiot's Guide to Body Language*. New York: Alpha, 2004.

Anderson, Laura Killen. *McGraw-Hill's Proofreading Handbook*. 2d ed. New York: McGraw-Hill, 2006.

Asher, Donald. *How to Get Any Job with Any Major: Career Launch & Re-launch for Everyone Under 30 or (How to Avoid Living in Your Parent's Basement)*. Berkeley, Calif.: Ten Speed Press, 2004.

Bachel, Beverly K. *What Do You Really Want? How to Set a Goal and Go for It! A Guide for Teens*. Minneapolis, Minn.: Free Spirit Publishing, 2001.

Ball, Michael. *You're Too Smart for This: Beating the 100 Big Lies About Your First Job*. Naperville, Ill.: Sourcebooks, 2006.

Baude, Dawn-Michelle. *The Executive Guide to E-mail Correspondence: Including Model Letters for Every Situation*. Franklin Lakes, N.J.: Career Press, 2006.

Beatty, Richard H. *175 High-Impact Cover Letters*. 3d ed. Hoboken, N.J: Wiley, 2008.

Blaustein, Arthur I. *Make a Difference: America's Guide to Volunteering and Community Service.* Rev. ed. San Francisco: Jossey-Bass, 2003.

Boldt, Arnold G. *No-Nonsense Job Interviews: How to Impress Prospective Employers and Ace Any Interview.* Franklin Lakes, N.J.: Career Press, 2008.

Bolles, Mark Emery, and Richard Nelson Bolles. *Job Hunting Online: A Guide to Using Job Listings, Message Boards, Research Sites, the Underweb, Counseling, InterNetworking Self-Assessment Tools, Niche Sites.* 5th ed. Berkeley, Calif.: Ten Speed Press, 2008.

Bolles, Richard Nelson. *What Color Is Your Parachute? 2009: A Practical Manual for Job-Hunters and Career-Changers.* Berkeley, Calif.: Ten Speed Press, 2008.

Bolles, Richard Nelson, Carol Christen, and Jean M. Blomquist. *What Color Is Your Parachute for Teens: Discovering Yourself, Defining Your Future.* Berkeley, Calif.: Ten Speed Press, 2006.

Camenson, Blythe. *Careers for Introverts & Other Solitary Types.* 2d ed. New York: McGraw-Hill, 2005.

Chapman, Jack. *Negotiating Your Salary: How to Make $1,000 a Minute.* 5th ed. Berkeley, Calif.: Ten Speed Press, 2006.

Clark, Roy Peter. *Writing Tools: 50 Essential Strategies for Every Writer.* New York: Little, Brown and Company, 2008.

Coplin, William D. *10 Things Employers Want You to Learn in College: The Know-How You Need to Succeed.* Berkeley, Calif.: Ten Speed Press, 2003.

Covey, Sean. *The 7 Habits of Highly Effective Teens.* New York: Fireside Press, 1998.

Covey, Stephen R. *The 7 Habits of Highly Effective People.* 15th ed. New York: The Free Press, 2004.

Damp, Dennis V., Robert A. Juran, and Salvatori Concialdi. *The Book of U.S. Government Jobs: Where They Are, What's Available & How to Get One.* 10th ed. McKees Rocks, Pa.: Bookhaven Press, 2008.

Darling, Diane. *Networking for Career Success.* New York: McGraw-Hill, 2005.

———. *The Networking Survival Guide: Get the Success You Want by Tapping Into the People You Know.* New York: McGraw-Hill, 2003.

Decker, Diane C., Victoria A. Hoevemeyer, and Marianne Rowe-Dimas. *First-Job Survival Guide: How to Thrive and Advance in Your New Career.* Indianapolis, Ind.: JIST Works, 2006.

DeLuca, Matthew J., and Nanette F. DeLuca. *Perfect Phrases for Negotiating Salary and Job Offers: Hundreds of Ready-to-Use Phrases to Help You Get the Best Possible Salary, Perks or Promotion.* New York: McGraw-Hill, 2006.

Dresser, Norine. *Multicultural Manners: Essential Rules of Etiquette for the 21st Century.* Rev. ed. Hoboken, N.J.: Wiley, 2005.

Editors of The American Heritage Dictionaries. *100 Words Almost Everyone Confuses and Misuses.* Boston: Houghton Mifflin, 2004.

————. *100 Words Every High School Graduate Should Know.* Boston: Houghton Mifflin, 2003.

Eikleberry, Carol, and Richard Nelson Bolles. *Career Guide for Creative and Unconventional People.* 3d ed. Berkeley, Calif.: Ten Speed Press, 2007.

Enelow, Wendy S., and Louise Kursmark. *Cover Letter Magic: Trade Secrets of Professional Resume Writers.* 3d ed. Indianapolis, Ind.: JIST Works, 2006.

Farr, Michael. *The Quick Resume & Cover Letter Book: Write and Use an Effective Resume in Only One Day.* 4th ed. Indianapolis, Ind.: JIST Works, 2007.

Fedorko, Jamie, and Dwight Allott. *The Intern Files: How to Get, Keep, and Make the Most of Your Internship.* New York: Simon Spotlight Entertainment, 2006.

Fox, Sue. *Etiquette For Dummies.* 2d ed. Hoboken, N.J.: For Dummies, 2007.

Freedman, Elizabeth. *Work 101: Learning the Ropes of the Workplace Without Hanging Yourself.* New York: Bantam Books, 2007.

Gay, Kathlyn. *Volunteering: The Ultimate Teen Guide.* Lanham, Md.: The Scarecrow Press, 2007.

Gilad, Suzanne. *Copyediting & Proofreading For Dummies.* Hoboken, N.J.: For Dummies, 2007.

Goldberg, Jan. *Careers for Extroverts & Other Gregarious Types.* 2d ed. New York: McGraw-Hill, 2005.

Gookin, Dan. *PCs For Dummies.* 11th ed. Hoboken, N.J.: For Dummies, 2007.

Greene, Brenda. *Get the Interview Every Time: Fortune 500 Hiring Professionals' Tips for Writing Winning Resumes and Cover Letters.* New York: Kaplan Business, 2004.

Griffin, Jack. *How to Say It at Work: Power Words, Phrases, and Communication Secrets for Getting Ahead.* 2d ed. Upper Saddle River, N.J.: Prentice Hall Press, 2008.

Hansen, Dhawn, and Tracey Turner. *Organize Your Office and Manage Your Time: A Be Smart Girls Guide.* Bloomington, Ind.: iUniverse Inc., 2007.

Hansen, Katherine. *A Foot in the Door: Networking Your Way into the Hidden Job Market.* Rev. ed. Berkeley, Calif.: Ten Speed Press, 2008.

Henderson, Veronique, and Pat Henshaw. *Image Matters for Men: How to Dress for Success!* London: Hamlyn, 2007.

Ireland, Susan. *The Complete Idiot's Guide to the Perfect Resume.* 4th ed. New York: Alpha, 2006.

Jovin, Ellen. *E-Mail Etiquette for Business Professionals.* New York: Syntaxis Press, 2007.

Kaip, Sarah. *The Woman's Workplace Survival Guide.* Medford, Oreg.: Advantage Source, 2005.

Kennedy, Joyce Lain. *Cover Letters For Dummies.* Hoboken, N.J.: For Dummies, 2009.

——. *Resumes For Dummies.* 5th ed. Hoboken, N.J.: For Dummies, 2007.

Klaus, Peggy. *The Hard Truth About Soft Skills: Workplace Lessons Smart People Wish They'd Learned Sooner.* New York: Collins Business, 2008.

Krannich, Ron. *Give Me More Money! Smart Salary Negotiation Tips for Getting Paid What You're Really Worth.* Manassas Park, Va.: Impact Publications, 2008.

Landy, Sylvia I. *Ditch the Flip-Flops: Ace Your Job Interview Fresh Out of College.* Winnetka, Ill.: Keystone Three LLC, 2007.

Langford, Beverly. *The Etiquette Edge: The Unspoken Rules for Business Success.* New York: AMACOM Books, 2005.

Lenius, Oscar. *A Well-Dressed Gentleman's Pocket Guide.* London: Prion, 2006.

Lerner, Dick. *Dress Like the Big Fish: How to Achieve the Image You Want and the Success You Deserve.* Omaha, Neb.: Bel Air Fashions Press, 2008.

Levine, John R., Margaret Levine Young, and Carol Baroudi. *The Internet For Dummies.* 11th ed. Hoboken, N.J.: For Dummies, 2007.

Levit, Alexandra. *How'd You Score That Gig?: A Guide to the Coolest Jobs (and How to Get Them).* New York: Ballantine Books, 2008.

Liang, Jengyee. *Hello Real World! A Student's Approach to Great Internships, Co-Ops, and Entry Level Positions.* Charleston, S.C.: BookSurge, 2006.

Medley, H. Anthony. *Sweaty Palms: The Neglected Art of Being Interviewed.* Manassas Park, Va.: Business Plus, 2005.

Miller, Patrick W. *Body Language on the Job.* Munster, Ind.: Patrick W. Miller & Associates, 2006.

Noble, David F. *Gallery of Best Cover Letters: Collection of Quality Cover Letters by Professional Resume Writers.* 3d ed. Indianapolis, Ind.: JIST Works, 2007.

Oldman, Mark. *Vault Guide to Top Internships, 2008 Edition.* Rev. ed. New York: Vault Inc., 2008.

Peres, Daniel. *Details Men's Style Manual: The Ultimate Guide for Making Your Clothes Work for You.* New York: Gotham, 2007.

Peterson, Robert R. *Landing the Internship or Full-Time Job During College.* Bloomington, Ind.: iUniverse Inc., 2005.

Piotrowski, Katy. *The Career Coward's Guide to Interviewing: Sensible Strategies for Overcoming Job Search Fears.* Indianapolis, Ind.: JIST Works, 2007.

Plotnik, Arthur. *Spunk & Bite: A Writer's Guide to Bold, Contemporary Style.* New York: Random House Reference, 2007.

Pollak, Lindsey. *Getting from College to Career: 90 Things to Do Before You Join the Real World.* New York: Collins Business, 2007.

Princeton Review. *The Internship Bible.* 10th ed. New York: Princeton Review, 2004.

Reiman, Tonya. *The Power of Body Language.* New York: Pocket, 2007.

Rosenberg, Bob, and Guy Lampard. *Giving from Your Heart: A Guide to Volunteering.* Bloomington, Ind.: iUniverse Inc., 2005.

Rozakis, Laurie E. *The Complete Idiot's Guide to Grammar and Style.* 2d ed. New York: Alpha, 2003.

Seligson, Hannah. *New Girl On the Job: Advice from the Trenches.* New York: Citadel, 2007.

Shatkin, Laurence. *200 Best Jobs for Introverts.* Indianapolis, Ind.: JIST Works, 2007.

Shertzer, Margaret. *The Elements of Grammar.* Reading, Mass.: Longman, 1996.

Simons, Warren, and Rose Curtis. *The Resume.Com Guide to Writing Unbeatable Resumes.* New York: McGraw-Hill, 2004.

Sindell, Milo, and Thuy Sindell. *Sink or Swim! New Job. New Boss. 12 Weeks to Get It Right.* 2d ed. Cincinnati, Ohio: Adams Media, 2006.

Song, Mike, Vicki Halsey, Tim Burress, and Ken Blanchard. *The Hamster Revolution: How to Manage Your Email Before It Manages You.* San Francisco: Berrett-Koehler Publishers, 2007.

Starry, Carolyn. *Surviving the Business Lunch: 25 Tips in 25 Minutes.* West Conshohocken, Pa.: Infinity Publishing, 2003.

Strunk, William Jr., and E. B. White. *The Elements of Style.* 4th ed. Boston: Allyn & Beacon, 2000.

Tieger, Paul D., and Barbara Barron. *Do What You Are: Discover the Perfect Career for You Through the Secrets of Personality Type.* Rev. ed. New York: Little, Brown and Company, 2007.

Tullier, Michelle. *Networking for Job Search and Career Success.* 2d ed. Indianapolis, Ind.: JIST Works, 2004.

University of Chicago. *The Chicago Manual of Style: The Essential Guide for Writers, Editors, and Publishers.* 15th ed. Chicago: The University of Chicago Press, 2003.

Van Devender, John, and Gloria Van Devender-Graves. *Savvy Interviewing: How to Ace the Interview & Get the Job.* Sterling, Va.: Capital Books, 2007.

Wallace, Richard. *The Only Resume and Cover Letter Book You'll Ever Need: 600 Resumes for All Industries, 600 Cover Letters for Every Situation, 150 Positions from Entry Level to CEO.* Cincinnati, Ohio: Adams Media, 2008.

Wegerbauer, Maryanne. *Next-Day Salary Negotiation: Prepare Tonight to Get Your Best Pay Tomorrow (Help in a Hurry).* Indianapolis, Ind.: JIST Works, 2007.

Weingarten, Rachel C. *Career and Corporate Cool.* Hoboken, N.J.: Wiley, 2007.

White, William J. *From Day One: CEO Advice to Launch an Extraordinary Career.* Upper Saddle River, N.J.: Prentice Hall, 2005.

Yate, Martin. *Knock 'em Dead Cover Letters.* 8th ed. Cincinnati: Adams Media, 2008.

Zichy, Shoya, and Ann Bidou. *Career Match: Connecting Who You Are With What You'll Love to Do.* New York: AMACOM Books, 2007.

Index